Tammy

MW01487390

BUILDING ON THE FOUNDATION

The WORD Building System

SECOND EDITION

LARRY HENDERSON JR.

OMINION

HBG

ISBN-13: 978-1731011763

ISBN-10: 1731011763

Published by Henderson Business Group (HBG), Intl.

Dedications

THANK YOU to The Kingdom Advancement Center, my family, and the many generations of Kingdom Institute students, past and present, who have dedicated their lives to getting wisdom and understanding from the Scriptures.

Your zeal to know the Word of God has continued to fuel me to strive to higher heights in Jesus Christ and to receive revelation to equip future generations for a life of Kingdom service. Your faith work is the driving force behind the release of this 2nd Edition of ***Building On The Foundation: The Word Building System***.

May you forever be dedicated to "Teaching the Word, Perfecting the Saints, Advancing the Kingdom of God!"

Table of Contents

Purpose

*For no one can lay any foundation other than the one
already laid, which is Jesus Christ. (I Corinthians 3:11
NIV)*

*Then was Jesus led up of the Spirit into the wilderness to
be tempted of the devil. And when He had fasted forty days
and forty nights, He was afterward an hungered. And
when the tempter came to Him, he said, If Thou be the Son
of God, command that these stones be made bread. But He
answered and said, It is written, Man shall not live by
bread alone, but by every word that proceedeth out of the
mouth of God. (Matthew 4:1-4)*

This is a most awesome statement of the Master: that
man shall live by every word that proceeds out of the mouth
of God. It means that everything we endeavor to do, say or
think in our lives should be based on the Word, every word
of our Father God.

There are two basic reasons I have written this book.
First, it is my utmost desire that every believer intimately
know the Word of God. I have made the following
statement many times and hope that I will get to say it a
million more; "The extent to which you know the Word of
God is the extent to which you will know God Himself,
because God is the Word." The Bible says, *"In the beginning
was the Word, and the Word was with God, and the Word was
God"* (John 1:1).

Want to know God? Get into His Word. All the wisdom we will ever need is found within the Word of God (Proverbs 15:33). Salvation is in the Word (Romans 10:13). Healing is in the Word (Psalm 103:3). Prosperity is in the Word (Deuteronomy 8:18). Faith is in the Word (Mark 11:22-23). Everything we will ever need is in the Word. Why? Because God is the Word and He is all we'll ever need (Acts 17:28).

The second purpose for which I have written this book is to cause every believer to have a ready, quick command of the Word of God. We need the kind of command that causes enemies to flee, the lame to walk, the sinner saved, the blind to see, and mountains to move whenever they hear a believer speak the Scriptures out of a heart filled with the Word of God.

Christ demonstrated this power to speak the Word of God with authority when tempted by the adversary. He was able to defeat the enemy and cause him to flee by simply speaking the Word (Matthew 4:10-11). But how was Jesus able to do this? He was able to defeat the adversary and walk in victory because He knew the uncompromising Word of God for His situation. He had taken the time previous to this trial to memorize and internalize the Word of God and deposit it into His heart (Luke 2:46-52).

Hebrews 5:14 says, *"But solid food is for the mature, who by constant use have trained themselves to distinguish good from evil."* (NIV) When we, as believers, equip ourselves with the Word of God, we are building on the foundation of Jesus Christ, the ability to speak the Word of God and receive supernatural results. Jesus said, *"If ye abide in me, and my words abide in you, ye shall ask what ye will, and it shall be done unto you"* (John 15:7). There is nothing that we cannot accomplish living by the words of Christ.

A Note to Pastors & Church Leaders

It was He who gave some apostles, some to be prophets, some to be evangelists, and some to be pastors and teachers, to prepare God's people for works of service, so that the Body of Christ may be built up until we all reach unity in the faith and in the knowledge of the Son of God and become mature, attaining to the whole measure of the fulness of Christ. (Ephesians 4:11-13 NIV)

Dear Pastor or Church Leader,

Many times, as overseers of the flock of God, it becomes difficult to minister to the people of God in the most effective way, because many members (including leaders) do not possess a working knowledge of the Word of God. As a result, many believers become discouraged and fall by the wayside because they are unable to fully grasp God's truths for their lives (Matthew 13:18-23). God said, *"My people are destroyed for lack of knowledge"* (Hosea 4:6a).

Another challenge facing the Church is the urgent need to effectively educate new believers after they have accepted Christ. I have often seen new believers fall through the cracks (in large and small Churches, alike), because they are not equipped immediately after the salvation experience with the necessary tools to be victorious, when they receive the Word of God. I have too often seen the Bibles of newly born-again believers left in pews, church offices, Sunday school rooms, or on dusty shelves, because the owner hasn't the slightest clue as to where they should begin in such an enormous book. It is for these reasons that I have been led to write *Building On The Foundation: The Word Building System.*

The Word Building System is a comprehensive approach to planting the living and active truth of the Scriptures in the heart of the believer. When used correctly, it is a ready companion to the Bible, suitable to build up the Body of Christ in faith, hope and the love of God that only comes through knowing His Word (Psalm 119:97). *The Word Building System* is designed to give the believer a firm foundation, rooted and grounded in the Word of God.

In addition, *The Word Building System* is an excellent church growth tool. *Building On The Foundation* is a superb supplement for Group Bible Studies, Marriage classes, Youth Groups, Sunday school, Bible Institutes and individual Bible study. It is the perfect tool to bring large fellowships closer and more intimate, as well as cause smaller fellowships to expand, as believers develop meaningful relationships with one another, experiencing the power of the Word of God together.

It is my hope, that every child of God will be blessed as they begin the journey of "building on the foundation" of Jesus Christ (1 Corinthians 3:11).

Sincerely,

Larry Henderson, Jr.

The Word Building System

The Word Building System is a comprehensive approach to training the believer to memorize, and thus, internalize the Word of God. It is designed to cause the user to be able to recite verses of Scripture from memory through a series of systematic memory reinforcements. This process, when coupled with regular Church involvement, Bible study, prayer and Holy Spirit conviction, is able to empower every child of God to have power over the enemy and to be victorious in every area of life regardless of the situation or circumstance.

In addition, *The Word Building System* is also designed to give the user understanding and insight into the mystery of the Word of God itself. Not only will the user internalize the Scriptures, but also gain an understanding of the Word which will make it easier to remember (Proverbs 4:7). Further details of how to use *The Word Building System* are explained in the "Instructions" and "A Few Guidelines" sections of this book.

Instructions

<u>Choose a Covenant Partner (CP)</u>

Before beginning this book, it is good to choose a Covenant Partner ("CP"). Your CP is someone who will be available to listen to you and help you grow as you study the Word of God within this book. Your CP can be a relative, a good friend, a business partner, a spouse, a fellow church member, a significant other, or anyone with whom you can grow in Christ.

The purpose for having your CP sign each memorized section is to give you an accomplishment as you move along this wonderful journey of knowing Our Father through His written Word! How often do we begin a worthy task for the sake of building our relationship with God and grow weary mid-stream only to find ourselves washed up on the shores of self-pity and defeat? This is where your CP dives in and rescues you with lots of encouragement and love to keep you going to the finish!

Every signature is a victory! You can make it to the end!

How to Use This Book

1) Each section of this book is divided into topics that have a number of verses related to them within each section. For example:

Prayer

John 14:14 – If ye shall ask any thing in My name, I will do it.

John 15:7 – If ye abide in Me, and My words abide in you, ye shall ask what ye will, and it shall be done unto you.

CP's Signature _____ Date _____

---

2) Read everything in each section and **MEMORIZE** the verses given. Though each section may have many verses within it, only memorize the verses written with this format:

Romans 6:23 – For the wages of sin is death; but the gift of God is eternal life through Jesus Christ our Lord.

---

3) After you have memorized each verse, word for word, recite the verses, one by one, to your CP.

4) After your CP has heard you say **ALL** the verses in a particular section, word for word, then he/she should sign their **OWN** name and the date that you successfully recited the verses (see example below).

CP's Signature _Larry Henderson, Jr._____ Date _____
5/31/2018

A Few Guidelines

The following guidelines are meant to help you obtain the maximum benefit of *The Word Building System*. When you use it as suggested below, it builds on the foundation of Christ and plants the living and active Word of God into your heart (Hebrews 4:12 NIV).

As with any set of guidelines, follow them with the wisdom and love of Jesus Christ, not as binding rules made to condemn. Follow them as a master set of laws made to develop and minister to you as you are led by the Spirit of God (2 Corinthians 3:17).

1) You must say **EVERY WORD** in each Scripture, verbatim. You **SHOULD NOT** substitute your own words. Every word of the Scripture is important and has been ordained of God for the specific purpose for which He has designed it.

2) When your CP has heard you say each verse within a section **AT LEAST ONCE,** you can receive a signature. It is not necessary to recite a verse over again, after it has been said, in order to ensure that you have really memorized it. There are plenty of verses throughout this book to ensure that true memorization occurs.

3) If, while you are reciting verses, you temporarily forget the rest of a verse and have to "take a peek" at the book in order to help your memory, that is OK.

4) Your CP **IS ONLY ALLOWED** to tell you **ONE WORD** in each Scripture if you cannot remember the verse. You **DO NOT** have to restate all of the verses in the section if this happens. You are encouraged to take advantage of this guideline. Feel free to ask.

5) Your CP **IS ALLOWED** to tell you the chapter and verse of a Scripture (example: John 1:1) to help you recite it.

6) You **DO NOT** need to memorize each section in order. But, you **SHOULD NOT** go to the next chapter until you have received a signature for **EVERY** section within a chapter. However, if you are using this book as a text book for a formal class, be sure to follow your instructor.

7) You **DO NOT** need to say the Scriptures in each section in order, but you must say **ALL** of them.

8) You will find that you will see the same verse in different sections. You **SHOULD NOT** skip over the verse. You must say the verse again. This is called *The Word Building System* and will cause you to write the Word of God on your heart forever.

9) It **IS NOT** mandatory that you memorize the Scripture verses in the presence of your CP. You may memorize verses whenever you have time, before bed, on the train, at home, at church, during Sunday school, at Bible Study, wherever. Just find your CP when you feel you are ready to say your Scriptures.

10) You **DO NOT** have to get the same person to sign your book every time you wish to finish a section. Anyone who is willing to listen to you and will follow the previously mentioned guidelines of this book can be your CP.

(Note: If you cannot, for whatever reason, memorize the Scriptures in this book, feel free to read through it and let it be a blessing to your life; NO CONDEMNATION)!

Individual Guidelines

If you just cannot find a CP anywhere or if you believe this book will best benefit you by completing it on your own, then you may choose yourself as your own CP. Simply follow the written **INSTRUCTIONS** and **GUIDELINES** sections and sign each section with your own name.

Marriage, Engagement & Couples Guidelines

If you are married, engaged or a couple and you wish to be built-up together in Christ, this is the perfect book for you. Simply choose your mate as your CP (whether you know it or not, you have already done this) and follow the written **INSTRUCTIONS** and **GUIDELINES** sections, with a few exceptions:

1) Keep the same CP throughout the duration of this book.

2) Get another book for your CP so that they can memorize verses also. You will find that going through this book together is the perfect way to build upon your relationship together. This will cause your relationship to have a foundation in the Word of God and nothing will be able to stop you from accomplishing God's will for your lives.

3) You **DO NOT** need to choose your mate as your CP for this book. But, it may be wise to finish this book with your mate if you start it with your mate. However, there is no need to be legalistic. You be the judge!

Part 1:
The Basics

Building On The Foundation

22

Chapter 1:
Salvation, Grace & Eternal Life

In the beginning, God made man to rule on the earth and have dominion over all things (Genesis 1:26-28). God put man (Adam) in the Garden of Eden, where he had everything he needed. At that time, man was prosperous in every area of his life. Adam had wealth, shelter, food, a beautiful wife (Eve), authority, a job (taking care of the Garden), and most of all, he walked unhindered with the Living God.

In Genesis Chapter 3, Adam forfeited all of this by submitting to the devil and taking a bite out of a fruit from the tree of the Knowledge of Good and Evil. This was the one thing God told him he should not do (Genesis 2:16-17). In the end, Adam eventually died unfulfilled and without an unhindered relationship with his God.

Because Adam sinned, every one of us who was born after him was born into sin. Consequently, all of us today spend most of our lives trying to regain everything that man was freely given in the Garden: wealth, a house, groceries, a beautiful woman (or rich man), authority on our job, and some clue about God's purpose for our lives.

Because Adam sinned, man was forever lost and separated from a personal relationship with his God. Man was sentenced to a life of defeat, slavery and toil. He now had to search for his purpose and his Creator.

Because God loves us, He sent His only Son, Jesus Christ, to die for our sins. He defeated sin and death on the Cross

behalf. He did for us what we could not do for ourselves. By His grace, He saved us from the power of sin and death to which Adam submitted in the Garden. The Bible says it this way:

But God demonstrates His own love for us in this: while we were still sinners, Christ died for us. (Romans 5:8 NIV)

Christ redeemed mankind from sin, death and destruction. All we must do to receive this gift is to accept the sacrifice of Jesus and allow Him to be Lord in our lives.

Now once again, man can have dominion on the earth, all of his needs met, an awesome spouse, and walk unhindered in the presence of the Living God through our Lord Jesus Christ. Hallelujah, we are saved!

<u>John 3:16</u> – For God so loved the world, that He gave His only begotten Son, that whosoever believeth in Him should not perish, but have everlasting life.

Begotten – Only born, as from a woman, from the womb (John 3:16).

<u>Romans 10:13</u> – For whosoever shall call upon the name of the Lord shall be saved.

CP's Signature _____ Date _____

Grace

<u>Ephesians 2:8-9</u> – For by grace are ye saved through faith; and that not of yourselves: it is the gift of God: not of works, lest any man should boast.

<u>2 Corinthians 9:8</u> – And God is able to make all grace abound to you, so that in all things at all times, having all that you need, you will abound in every good work. (NIV)

Grace – Unearned favor or kindness, unmerited gift (Ephesians 2:8-9); special abundance or blessing, provision (2 Corinthians 9:8, 12:9); a time of forgiveness, as with debt (Ephesians 1:7); a grace period.

CP's Signature _____ Date _____

Assurance

<u>Psalm 27:1</u> – The LORD is my light and my salvation; whom shall I fear? The LORD is the strength of my life; of whom shall I be afraid?

CP's Signature _____ Date _____

Jesus is Lord

<u>Romans 10:9</u> – That if you confess with your mouth, "Jesus is Lord," and believe in your heart that God raised Him from the dead, you will be saved. (NIV)

<u>Romans 10:10</u> – For it is with your heart that you believe and are justified, and it is with your mouth that you confess and are saved. (NIV)

CP's Signature _____ Date _____

The Gift of God

Romans 3:23 – For all have sinned, and come short of the glory of God.

Romans 6:23 – For the wages of sin is death; but the gift of God is eternal life through Jesus Christ our Lord.

CP's Signature _____ Date _____

God's Love Toward Us

Romans 5:8 – But God commendeth His love toward us, in that, while we were yet sinners, Christ died for us.

> **Commendeth** – Demonstrates or shows (Romans 5:8).

Romans 5:9 – Much more then, being now justified by His blood, we shall be saved from wrath through Him.

> **Justified** – To be reinstated into right-standing before God because of the sacrifice of Christ (Romans 5:1,9); when God has made it **just-as-if-I'd** never sinned (1 Corinthians 6:11).

> **Salvation (Saved)** – Deliverance or rescue (Genesis 49:18; Psalm 37:39); preserved or restored back to the original position or state (Psalm 14:7; Luke 1:76-77); God has saved us from the penalty of sin (Acts 4:12; Romans 1:16, 6:23), and has caused us to be seated in heavenly places with Christ Jesus (Ephesians 2:6); when we are saved, we regain the original authority that God gave Adam in the beginning, to rule and reign over the earth (Genesis 1:26-28; John 1:12).

1 John 4:10 – Herein is love, not that we loved God, but that He loved us, and sent His Son to be the propitiation for our sins.

> **Propitiation** – Atoning sacrifice, payment for wrongdoing (Romans 3:25); acceptable substitute (1 John 2:2).

CP's Signature _____ Date _____

Choosing the Son & Life (Part 1)

John 11:25 – Jesus said unto her, I am the resurrection, and the life: he that believeth in Me, though he were dead, yet shall he live.

John 14:6 – Jesus said unto him, I am the Way, the Truth, and the Life: no man cometh unto the Father, but by Me.

John 20:31 – But these are written, that ye might believe that Jesus is the Christ, the Son of God; and that believing ye might have life through His name.

1 John 5:12 – He that hath the Son hath life; and he that hath not the Son of God hath not life.

CP's Signature _____ Date _____

Choosing the Son & Life (Part 2)

John 8:12 – Then spake Jesus again unto them, saying, I am the light of the world: he that followeth Me shall not walk in darkness, but shall have the light of life.

John 10:10 – The thief cometh not, but for to steal, and to kill, and to destroy: I am come that they might have life, and that they might have it more abundantly.

Romans 5:17 – For if by one man's offense, death reigned by one; much more they which receive abundance of grace and of the gift of righteousness shall reign in life by One, Jesus Christ.

Galatians 2:20 – I am crucified with Christ: nevertheless, I live; yet not I, but Christ liveth in me: and the life which I now live in the flesh, I live by the faith of the Son of God, who loved me, and gave Himself for me.

CP's Signature _____ Date _____

No Condemnation – No Shame

Once we have received Christ, the Word of God tells us there is no condemnation. When something is condemned, it is declared to be uninhabitable, unfit, of no value, and suitable only to be discarded and burned.

Many times, when we sin after we have received Christ, the devil tries to convince us we are not really saved. He tries to condemn us, so we will think God no longer inhabits our lives and we are of no value to Him. He wants us to think that God no longer desires to use us for His good purpose.

However, the Bible says: *"whom the Son sets free is free, indeed"* (John 8:36). Jesus said He would lose not one of all the Father gives Him (John 6:39). A just man falls seven times, yet gets back up again (Proverbs 24:16). God desires to finish the good work He started in you, the day you received Jesus as Lord (Philippians 1:6).

No condemnation means just what it says: your finances are not condemned, your health is not condemned, your family is not condemned, and your resources are not condemned. The devil no longer has the authority to do what he wants to do in your life. Christ has set you free, indeed. Go get the job God has for you. Receive the promotion God has for you. Get the husband God has for you. Take hold of the wealth God has stored up for you. Take the vacation God has ordained for you. Go to the school God has established for you. Walk in the ministry God has called you to. You no longer have to live a defeated life. There is no condemnation!

John 3:17 – For God sent not His Son into the world to condemn the world; but that the world through Him might be saved.

John 3:18 – He that believeth on Him is not condemned: but he that believeth not is condemned already, because he hath not believed in the name of the only begotten Son of God.

Romans 8:1 – There is therefore now no condemnation to them which are in Christ Jesus, who walk not after the flesh, but after the Spirit.

Romans 10:11 – For the Scripture saith, Whosoever believeth on Him shall not be ashamed.

CP's Signature _____ Date _____

Eternal Life (Part 1)

John 10:27-28 – My sheep hear My voice, and I know them, and they follow Me: and I give unto them eternal life; and they shall never perish, neither shall any man pluck them out of My hand.

John 17:3 – And this is life eternal, that they might know Thee, the only true God, and Jesus Christ, whom Thou hast sent.

Romans 6:23 – For the wages of sin is death; but the gift of God is eternal life through Jesus Christ our Lord.

CP's Signature _____ Date _____

Eternal Life (Part 2)

1 John 5:11 – And this is the record, that God hath given to us eternal life, and this life is in His Son.

1 John 5:13 – These things have I written unto you that believe on the name of the Son of God; that ye may know that ye have eternal life, and that ye may believe on the name of the Son of God.

1 John 5:20 – And we know that the Son of God is come, and hath given us an understanding, that we may know Him that is true, and we are in Him that is true, even in His Son Jesus Christ. This is the true God, and eternal life.

CP's Signature _____ Date _____

The Sacrifice of Christ

John 3:16 – For God so loved the world, that He gave His only begotten Son, that whosoever believeth in Him should not perish, but have everlasting life.

Romans 5:8-9 – But God commendeth His love toward us, in that, while we were yet sinners, Christ died for us. Much more then, being now justified by His blood, we shall be saved from wrath through Him.

2 Corinthians 5:21 – For He hath made Him to be sin for us, who knew no sin; that we might be made the righteousness of God in Him.

1 John 2:2 – And He is the propitiation for our sins: and not for ours only, but also for the sins of the whole world.

CP's Signature _____ Date _____

The Plan of Salvation

(What must we do to be saved?)

Romans 10:8b-10 – "... The word is near you; it is in your mouth and in your heart," that is, the word of faith we are proclaiming: that if you confess with your mouth, "Jesus is Lord," and believe in your heart that God raised Him from the dead, you will be saved. For it is with your heart that you believe and are justified, and it is with your mouth that you confess and are saved. (NIV)

Revelation 3:20 – Behold, I stand at the door, and knock: if any man hear My voice, and open the door, I will come in to him, and will sup with him, and he with Me.

When Jesus died and rose from the dead, having never sinned, He defeated sin and death once and for all and gained all power in heaven and earth (Matthew 28:18), becoming King of kings and Lord of lords (Revelation 19:16). Now that Jesus is King, all that we must do in order to be saved from the power of sin and death is to confess that "Jesus is Lord" and we will have the right to enter into the Kingdom of God and be saved (John 1:12-13).

If you have not yet accepted Jesus as Lord and you believe that Jesus died for your sins (Romans 3:23, 5:8, 6:23) and was raised from the dead (Acts 13:30), so you could have eternal life (John 3:16), simply confess with your mouth "Jesus is Lord," and you shall be saved (Romans 10:9-10).

Welcome to the family of God! Go on to Chapter 2 so that you can learn how to pray and Study the Bible. Praise God, Jesus is Lord!!!!

CP's Signature _____ Date _____

Chapter 2:
Bible Study, Prayer & Some Other Things

The most fundamental tools in the life of every Christian are prayer and Bible study. This is true much the same way that the fundamental tools of a carpenter are a hammer and nail; without them, he just simply cannot do his job. In order to be effective and successful, Christians must master the arts of prayer and Bible study. As you memorize the Scriptures in this chapter, meditate on their meanings and what God would have you to do to build on your foundation in Him.

<u>Find a Place for Prayer</u>

Jesus instructed His disciples to enter into their closet, shut the door and pray to the Father who is in secret ... and He will reward openly (Matthew 6:5-6). Find a quiet place where you can get into God's presence without distraction.

Pray out loud. Have a prayer list (of things for which to pray). It is not essential that you pray with your eyes closed; however, this may help your intimacy and concentration. All these things will keep you from being distracted. Remember, the enemy knows the power of prayer and will use any means necessary to prevent you from praying.

Matthew 6:6 – But thou, when thou prayest, enter into thy closet, and when thou hast shut thy door, pray to thy Father which is in secret; and thy Father which seeth in secret shall reward thee openly.

CP's Signature _____ Date _____

Study the Bible Prayerfully

In order to study the Bible, we must precede Bible Study with prayer. Because all Scripture is God-breathed, we must consult the author, God, to fully understand it. Only the Spirit of God knows the thoughts of God (1 Corinthians 2:10-11). We have the mind of Christ (1 Corinthians 2:16).

<u>2 Timothy 3:16</u> – All Scripture is given by inspiration of God, and is profitable for doctrine, for reproof, for correction, for instruction in righteousness.

CP's Signature _____ Date _____

Set a Time for Prayer

Jesus prayed early in the morning, before the day began, in a solitary place (Mark 1:35). The morning is, by far, the best time to pray. Even David prayed in the morning (Psalm 5:3). The fewest distractions are in the morning, before work, class or before the kids get up (or your parents, for that matter).

If you desire to have an intimate relationship with the Father, get up early in the morning. This will show your commitment and sincerity to be with Him. You will find that a few minutes of lost sleep is the perfect offering to God.

Also set times to pray throughout the day. Daniel prayed three times a day (Daniel 6:10). The psalmist praised seven times a day (Psalm 119:164). Remember to pray without ceasing (1 Thessalonians 5:17). Pray in the car, for the sick when you see a hospital, the bereaved when you see a funeral home, passengers in an accident, pray for children when you see a school, etc. Always be ready to pray (Ephesians 6:18).

Isaiah 50:4 – The LORD God hath given me the tongue of the learned, that I should know how to speak a word in season to him that is weary: He wakeneth morning by morning, He wakeneth mine ear to hear as the learned.

CP's Signature _____ Date _____

Prayer and the Word

John 14:14 – If ye shall ask any thing in My name, I will do it.

John 15:7 – If ye abide in Me, and My words abide in you, ye shall ask what ye will, and it shall be done unto you.

CP's Signature _____ Date _____

What to Study?

Study to show yourself approved. Simply reading the Scriptures is not studying them. It is a good idea to choose a subject to study, such as love, trust, temptation or salvation. It is also a good idea to study just one book of the Bible (i.e., John or Romans). You can use this book to study. Ask God what you should study, and He will lead you by His Spirit (John 14:26). Seek after wisdom and understanding.

Proverbs 4:7 – Wisdom is the principal thing; therefore, get wisdom: and with all thy getting, get understanding.

2 Timothy 2:15 Study to show thyself approved unto God, a workman that needeth not to be ashamed, rightly dividing the word of truth.

CP's Signature _____ Date 2/10/20

Increased Expectation in Prayer

Ephesians 3:20 – Now unto Him that is able to do exceeding abundantly above all that we ask or think, according to the power that worketh in us.

1 John 5:14-15 – And this is the confidence that we have in Him, that, if we ask any thing according to His will, He heareth us: and if we know that He hear us, whatsoever we ask, we know that we have the petitions that we desired of Him.

CP's Signature _____ Date _____

Ask and Receive

Matthew 7:7 – Ask, and it shall be given you; seek, and ye shall find; knock, and it shall be opened unto you.

Matthew 7:8 – For every one that asketh receiveth; and he that seeketh findeth; and to him that knocketh it shall be opened.

Matthew 21:22 – And all things, whatsoever ye shall ask in prayer, believing, ye shall receive.

CP's Signature _____ Date _____

All the Word

The Bible says: *"those things which are revealed belong unto us and to our children forever"* (Deuteronomy 29:29). Within the Bible is the revealed Word of God. If this is true, then the Word of God literally belongs to us, we own it and have title to it. It is our job to maintain and cultivate the Word of God in our lives as our purchased possession.

Therefore, as the People of God we have but one obligation, to figure out the will of God through His Word, believe it and do it.

Deuteronomy 29:29 – The secret things belong unto the LORD our God: but those things which are revealed belong unto us and to our children for ever, that we may do all the words of this law.

Joshua 1:8 – This book of the law shall not depart out of thy mouth; but thou shall meditate therein day and night, that thou mayest observe to do according to all that is written therein: for then thou shalt make thy way prosperous, and then thou shalt have good success.

CP's Signature _____ Date _____

Trust In the Lord

Psalms 37:23-24 – The steps of a good man are ordered by the LORD: and he delighteth in his way. Though he fall, he shall not be utterly cast down: for the LORD upholdeth him with His hand.

Proverbs 3:5-6 – Trust in the LORD with all thine heart; and lean not unto thine own understanding. In all thy ways acknowledge Him, and He shall direct thy paths.

Proverbs 16:3 – Commit thy works unto the LORD, and thy thoughts shall be established.

CP's Signature _____ Date _____

The Will of God

Wouldn't life be easier if God would just tell us exactly what He wants us to do? All of us have asked ourselves the question "What is God's plan for my life," "What does God want me to do," or "What is the answer to my prayer?" We wish God would just come down and speak to us like He did with Moses, Joshua, David, Abraham, Paul, the disciples and many others in the Bible.

We long to rid ourselves of the empty stillness that we hear after we pray and replace it with the live voice of God. Is this so much to ask?

The mystery of getting our prayers answered and hearing God's voice when we speak to Him is solved in 1 John 5:14-15.

> *This is the confidence we have in approaching God: that if we ask anything according to His will, He hears us; and if we know that He hears us – whatever we ask – we know that we have what we asked of Him. (NIV)*

The concept of this verse is very simple: When you pray, ask God for what He wants to happen (His will) and He will always hear your prayer. If God hears your prayer, then He will always grant your request. This makes perfect sense. Anyone will gladly give you what you ask them, if you ask them for what they already said you can possess. Now, the only question is: "What is the will of God, so that I can always ask accordingly?"

Glad you asked! The Word of God is the will of God. When we read and study the Bible, we are reading the will of God, His Word. There are two ways we can find out someone's will:

1) By reading their written will (a written declaration concerning wealth dispersion to be activated upon one's death, Hebrews 9:16-17);

2) By listening to the words that they say (Luke 6:45).

Great news, we have both! The Bible is the written Word of God through Christ, who died for the sins of the world (John 1:29, Revelation 13:8). Here, prayer and Bible study go hand-in-hand. We read the Word of God to discover His will and we pray according to His will to guarantee that we will receive what we ask of Him. Wow, what a promise!

Here are two verses to help you realize God's will in your life:

Romans 12:1 – I beseech you therefore, brethren, by the mercies of God, that ye present your bodies a living sacrifice, holy, acceptable unto God, which is your reasonable service.

Romans 12:2 – And be not conformed to this world: but be ye transformed by the renewing of your mind, that ye may prove what is that good, and acceptable, and perfect will of God.

CP's Signature _____ Date _____

Be Obedient to the Word

After we have done all these things, we must be obedient to the Word. Faith without works is dead (James 2:17). We must receive the harvest of our obedience to the Word and bear fruit: some thirty, some sixty, some a hundredfold (Matthew 13:23; John 15:7-8, 16). Many times, God will not show us what He has in store for us in the future until we first are obedient to what He has told us in the present. Do what God has told you to do, and then He will show you what He wants to do next in your life.

Ecclesiastes 12:13 – Let us hear the conclusion of the whole matter: fear God and keep His commandments: for this is the whole duty of man.

James 1:22 – But be ye doers of the word, and not hearers only, deceiving your own selves.

CP's Signature _____ Date _____

A Guide in Prayer

To learn how to pray or decrease distraction and always stay on track in prayer, it is a good idea to use the acronym ACTS as a guide (think about the book of Acts in the New Testament).

- **Adoration** (Matt 6:9) – Always acknowledge God for who He is: Our Father. Jesus Himself used "Daddy" or "Abba" (Mark 14:36; also, Romans 8:15; Galatians 4:6). This is an awesome revelation to be able to call the Creator "Father." For every child knows that he can depend on his father to supply all of his needs (Philippians 4:19). The Bible says: *"Which of you, if his son asks for bread, will give him a stone? Or if he asks for a fish, will give him a snake? If you, then, though you are evil, know how to give good gifts to your children, how much more will your Father in heaven give good gifts to those who ask Him?"* (Matthew 7:9-11). Our Father is always ready to hear our requests and is anxious to supply our needs.

- **Confession** (I John 1:9) – When we confess our sins, we set our hearts free and overcome the guilt of sin (1 John 3:19-24). Psalm 66:18 says: *"If I regard iniquity in my heart,* *the LORD will not hear me."* Sin separates us from God (Galatians 5:19-21). When you pray, simply confess all your known sins to the Father or find a trusted brother or sister in Christ to confess your sins (James 5:16). He has promised to cleanse us from all unrighteousness (1 John 1:9).

- **T**hanksgiving (Philippians 4:6) – *"Do not be anxious about anything, but in everything, by prayer and petition, with thanksgiving, present your requests to God."* Always thank God for what He has done, what He is doing, and the awesome things He is about to do in your life.

- **S**upplication/Intercession (1 Timothy 2:1-2) – Lastly, pray for others first and then yourself. Supplications are our earnest pleas and requests to the Father. Intercession is prayer for others with the same urgency with which we would pray for ourselves. To intercede, we must put ourselves, figuratively speaking, in that person's shoes. Remember: Hebrews 4:15, 7:23-25; also, see Matthew 6:5-15.

James 5:14 – Is any sick among you? Let him call for the elders of the church; and let them pray over him, anointing him with oil in the name of the Lord.

James 5:15 – And the prayer of faith shall save the sick, and the Lord shall raise him up; and if he hath committed sins, they shall be forgiven him.

James 5:16 – Confess your faults one to another, and pray one for another, that ye may be healed. The effectual fervent prayer of a righteous man availeth much.

CP's Signature _____ Date _____

Fasting

Prayer must be accompanied with periodic fasting. Fasting loosens the enemies grip on our lives and allows us to operate in renewed belief. Believing by faith is necessary to be successful in spiritual warfare (Matthew 17:21). Fasting denies the flesh and allows our spirit man to dominate our lives, resulting in actions out of faith instead of fear.

<u>Isaiah 58:6</u> – Is not this the fast that I have chosen? To loose the bands of wickedness, to undo the heavy burdens, and to let the oppressed go free, and that ye break every yoke?

<u>Joel 1:14</u> – Sanctify ye a fast, call a solemn assembly, gather the elders and all the inhabitants of the land into the house of the LORD your God, and cry unto the LORD,

CP's Signature _____ Date _____

Fasting Correctly

<u>Matthew 6:16</u> – Moreover when ye fast, be not, as the hypocrites, of a sad countenance: for they disfigure their faces, that they may appear unto men to fast. Verily I say unto you, they have their reward.

<u>Matthew 6:17</u> – But thou, when thou fastest, anoint thine head, and wash thy face.

<u>Matthew 6:18</u> – That thou appear not unto men to fast, but unto thy Father which is in secret: and thy Father, which seeth in secret, shall reward thee openly.

CP's Signature _____ Date _____

Chapter 3:
Understanding the Kingdom of God

The most important subject in the Bible is God. However, the most important subject to God in the Bible is His Kingdom. Jesus commanded us to seek the Kingdom of God, first (Matthew 6:33). The entire Bible from Genesis to Revelation is about the Kingdom of God. It is about how God desires to establish His Kingdom on earth, as it is in Heaven (Matthew 6:9-10).

It is easy to conceptualize the Kingdom of God. *Kingdom* is a compound word. It is a combination of the words *King* and *Dominion*. This tells us the Kingdom is the place where the *King* has *Dominion*. More specifically, it is the place where the King has supreme rule, dominion and authority. Jesus Christ is King of kings and Lord of lords (Revelation 19:16).

The Kingdom First

Jesus commanded us to seek His Kingdom, first. Our number one mandate as Disciples of Christ is to do our part to cause His Kingdom to come on earth, as it is in Heaven.

There is no sickness in Heaven; therefore, we lay hands on the sick that they may be healed. There is no hate or selfishness in Heaven; therefore, we are commanded to Love. There is no poverty in Heaven; therefore, we are called to give. There is no devil in Heaven; therefore, we are called to make the enemies of Christ His footstool.

<u>Matthew 6:33</u> – But seek ye first the Kingdom of God, and His righteousness; and all these things shall be added unto you.

> **Kingdom** – The place where the King has supreme rule, dominion and authority (1 Corinthians 15:24).

CP's Signature _____ Date _____

The Kingdom Prayer

<u>Matthew 6:9</u> – After this manner therefore pray ye: Our Father which art in heaven, hallowed be Thy name.

<u>Matthew 6:10</u> – Thy Kingdom come. Thy will be done in earth, as it is in heaven.

<u>Matthew 6:11</u> – Give us this day our daily bread.

<u>Matthew 6:12</u> – And forgive us our debts, as we forgive our debtors.

<u>Matthew 6:13</u> – And lead us not into temptation, but deliver us from evil: for Thine is the Kingdom, and the power, and the glory, for ever. Amen.

CP's Signature _____ Date _____

Receiving an Inheritance

<u>Matthew 5:3</u> – Blessed are the poor in spirit: for theirs is the Kingdom of Heaven.

<u>Matthew 5:10</u> – Blessed are they which are persecuted for righteousness' sake: for theirs is the Kingdom of Heaven.

<u>1 Corinthians 15:50</u> – Now this I say, brethren, that flesh and blood cannot inherit the Kingdom of God; neither doth corruption inherit incorruption.

CP's Signature _____ Date _____

Without Observation

Jesus taught that the Kingdom of God cannot be observed with the natural eye (Luke 17:20). The Kingdom is not a physical but a spiritual kingdom (John 3:1-8). He taught that the Kingdom of God is within those that are His disciples. This means the place where Jesus has supreme rule, dominion and authority is within the hearts of those that have accepted Him as their personal Lord and Savior (Romans 10:8-10).

We are not to look for a physical kingdom. The Kingdom of God is wherever the saints are present. We are to be as salt in the earth, making an impact wherever we may go. We are to be a city on a hill that cannot be hidden. We are to let our light shine before men, so our lives bring glory to our Father in Heaven (Matthew 5:13-16).

<u>Luke 17:20</u> – And when He was demanded of the Pharisees, when the kingdom of God should come, He answered them and said, The Kingdom of God cometh not with observation:

Luke 17:21 – Neither shall they say, Lo here! or, lo there! for, behold, the Kingdom of God is within you.

CP's Signature _____ Date _____

Entering the Kingdom

Luke 18:17 – Verily I say unto you, Whosoever shall not receive the Kingdom of God as a little child shall in no wise enter therein.

Luke 18:25 – For it is easier for a camel to go through a needle's eye, than for a rich man to enter into the Kingdom of God.

John 3:3 – Jesus answered and said unto him, Verily, verily, I say unto thee, Except a man be born again, he cannot see the Kingdom of God.

John 3:5 – Jesus answered, Verily, verily, I say unto thee, Except a man be born of water and of the Spirit, he cannot enter into the Kingdom of God.

CP's Signature _____ Date _____

Defining the Kingdom

Romans 14:17 – For the Kingdom of God is not meat and drink; but righteousness, and peace, and joy in the Holy Ghost.

1 Corinthians 4:20 – For the Kingdom of God is not in word, but in power.

CP's Signature _____ Date _____

The Righteous of God

Matthew 6:33 – But seek ye first the Kingdom of God, and His righteousness; and all these things shall be added unto you.

Romans 14:17 – For the kingdom of God is not meat and drink; but righteousness, and peace, and joy in the Holy Ghost.

Matthew 5:10 – Blessed are they which are persecuted for righteousness' sake: for theirs is the Kingdom of Heaven.

CP's Signature _____ Date _____

Chapter 4:
Faith and the Word of God

The Word of God

Since the beginning of time, man has sought to discover and to know the Living God. When they thought the earth was flat, men tried to travel to the end of the earth or build towers up to heaven to find God (Genesis 11:1-9). However, the Bible clearly explains who God is and what we must possess to find Him, the Word.

The Bible says, *"In the beginning was the Word, and the Word was with God, and the Word was God"* (John 1:1). When we read and study the Word of God, we are literally getting to know God Himself and He is being revealed to us. There are some who say they have found God and know the Father, but do not know the Word. They are liars! It is impossible for us to know God apart from knowing His Word. Why? Because God IS the Word. Herein is the most awesome concept: to know God and to know His Word.

John 1:1-3 – In the beginning was the Word, and the Word was with God, and the Word was God. The same was in the beginning with God. All things were made by Him; and without Him was not any thing made that was made.

John 1:14 – And the Word was made flesh, and dwelt among us, (and we beheld His glory, the glory as of the only begotten of the Father) full of grace and truth.

John 15:7 – If ye abide in Me, and My words abide in you, ye shall ask what ye will, and it shall be done unto you.

Hebrews 4:12 – For the Word of God is quick, and powerful, and sharper than any two-edged sword, piercing even to the dividing asunder of soul and spirit, and of the joints and marrow, and is a discerner of the thoughts and intents of the heart.

CP's Signature _____ Date _____

Believing in the Son of God

John 1:12 – But as many as received Him, to them gave He power to become the sons of God, even to them that believe on His name.

John 3:18 – He that believeth on Him is not condemned: but he that believeth not is condemned already, because he hath not believed in the name of the only begotten Son of God.

1 John 5:12 – He that hath the Son hath life; and he that hath not the Son of God hath not life.

CP's Signature _____ Date _____

Faith

Mark 11:22b-23 – Have faith in God. For verily I say unto you, that whosoever shall say unto this mountain, Be thou removed, and be thou cast into the sea; and shall not doubt in his heart, but shall believe that those things which he saith shall come to pass; he shall have whatsoever he saith.

Hebrews 11:1 – Now faith is the substance of things hoped for, the evidence of things not seen.

Hebrews 11:6 – But without faith it is impossible to please Him: for he that cometh to God must believe that He is, and that He is a rewarder of them that diligently seek Him.

CP's Signature _____ Date _____

Meditate on the Word

One of the most important parts of the life of the believer is to meditate on God's Word. Meditation will help you memorize the Word and deposit it in your soul (Psalm 37:31, 119:11). The more the Word is being deposited in our hearts, the more we are becoming like God and know His will for our lives (Proverbs 23:7; Luke 6:45).

It is essential that we take the time to meditate on God's Word. God promises we will be like trees firmly planted by streams of water, our leaves shall not wither, and whatever we do shall prosper if we meditate on the Word (Psalm 1:3). To meditate on the Word is to meditate on the Will of God and literally become overtaken by God Himself, because He is the Word (John 1:1).

Psalm 1:1-2 – Blessed is the man that walketh not in the counsel of the ungodly, nor standeth in the way of sinners, nor sitteth in the seat of the scornful. But his delight is in the Law of the LORD; and in His Law doth he meditate day and night.

Joshua 1:8 – This book of the Law shall not depart out of thy mouth; but thou shall meditate therein day and night, that thou mayest observe to do according to all that is written therein: for then thou shalt make thy way prosperous, and then thou shalt have good success.

Psalm 19:14 – Let the words of my mouth, and the meditation of my heart, be acceptable in Thy sight, O LORD, my strength, and my Redeemer.

Psalm 119:15 – I will meditate in Thy precepts, and have respect unto Thy ways.

CP's Signature _____ Date _____

The Word & the Heart

Psalm 119:10 – With my whole heart have I sought Thee: O let me not wander from Thy commandments.

Psalm 119:11 – Thy Word have I hid in mine heart, that I might not sin against Thee.

Psalm 119:34 – Give me understanding, and I shall keep Thy Law; yea, I shall observe it with my whole heart.

CP's Signature _____ Date _____

Living According to the Word (Part 1)

Psalm 119:9 – How can a young man keep his way pure? By living according to Your Word. (NIV)

Psalm 119:105 – Thy Word is a lamp unto my feet, and a light unto my path.

Matthew 4:4 – But He answered and said, It is written, Man shall not live by bread alone, but by every word that proceedeth out of the mouth of God.

CP's Signature _____ Date _____

Only Believe

The most essential part of walking by faith is the extent to which we are able to accept what God has said and believe it wholeheartedly. Many times, we as believers want to believe the Word and say we believe it, but do not. We believe God is able to heal from cancer, but doubt if He really will heal our loved ones.

We know that Jesus told the man with the infirmity to *"Rise, take up thy bed, and walk,"* but doubt that He will do the same thing for the man we pass by in the wheelchair every Sunday (John 5:8). We believe God endowed believers to speak in other tongues in the Bible, but doubt that we are able to do the same thing today (Mark 16:17-18). In order to walk by faith, we must make up our minds that we are going to "believe only." Jesus said it best concerning the deceased daughter of Jairus, *"Fear not: **believe only**, and she shall be made whole"* (Luke 8:50).

"Only believing" means making a decision to refuse to think about or receive any other answers to our situation than receiving the promise of God. When we "only believe," we are guaranteed to receive what we ask for or do by faith. This kind of believing pleases God (Hebrews 11:6) and causes us to take hold of the Kingdom.

We must make a decision to remove from our lives those things that would cause us to doubt the truth of God's Word for our lives, so we will always be in a position to please God by faith and "only believe."

Matthew 21:22 – And all things, whatsoever ye shall ask in prayer, believing, ye shall receive.

Mark 9:23 – Jesus said unto him, If thou canst believe, all things are possible to him that believeth.

Mark 11:24 – Therefore I say unto you, What things soever ye desire, when ye pray, believe that ye receive them, and ye shall have them.

Mark 16:17, 18 – And these signs shall follow them that believe: in My name shall they cast out devils; they shall speak with new tongues; they shall take up serpents; and if they drink any deadly thing, it shall not hurt them; they shall lay hands on the sick, and they shall recover.

CP's Signature _____ Date _____

Living According to the Word (Part 2)

John 15:7 – If ye abide in Me, and My words abide in you, ye shall ask what ye will, and it shall be done unto you.

John 8:31b-32 – If ye continue in My Word, then are ye My disciples indeed; And ye shall know the truth, and the truth shall make you free.

Romans 10:17 – So then, faith cometh by hearing, and hearing by the Word of God.

1 Timothy 4:12 – Let not man despise thy youth; but be thou an example of the believers, in word, in conversation, in charity, in spirit, in faith, in purity.

2 Timothy 2:15 Study to show thyself approved unto God, a workman that needeth not to be ashamed, rightly dividing the word of truth.

CP's Signature _____ Date _____

Walking By Faith

Romans 1:17 – For therein is the righteousness of God revealed from faith to faith: as it is written, the just shall live by faith.

Romans 10:17 – So then, faith cometh by hearing, and hearing by the Word of God.

2 Corinthians 5:7 – For we walk by faith, not by sight.

CP's Signature _____ Date _____

Believing in His Name

<u>John 1:12</u> – But as many as received Him, to them gave He power to become the sons of God, even to them that believe on His name.

<u>John 3:18</u> – He that believeth on Him is not condemned: but he that believeth not is condemned already, because he hath not believed in the name of the only begotten Son of God.

<u>Acts 2:38</u> – Then Peter said unto them, Repent, and be baptized every one of you in the name of Jesus Christ for the remission of sins, and ye shall receive the gift of the Holy Ghost.

<u>Acts 4:12</u> – Neither is there salvation in any other: for there is none other name under heaven given among men, whereby we must be saved.

<u>Romans 10:13</u> – For whosoever shall call upon the name of the Lord shall be saved.

<u>1 John 3:23</u> – And this is His commandment, that we should believe on the name of His Son Jesus Christ, and love one another, as He gave us commandment.

CP's Signature _____ Date _____

There is Power in Jesus Name

<u>Mark 16:17,18</u> – And these signs shall follow them that believe: in My name shall they cast out devils; they shall speak with new tongues; they shall take up serpents; and if they drink any deadly thing it shall not hurt them; they shall lay hands on the sick, and they shall recover.

<u>John 14:14</u> – If ye shall ask any thing in My name, I will do it.

James 5:14-15 – Is any sick among you? Let him call for the elders of the church; and let them pray over him, anointing him with oil in the name of the Lord: and the prayer of faith shall save the sick, and the Lord shall raise him up; and if he have committed sins, they shall be forgiven him.

CP's Signature _____ Date _____

Speaking by Faith

Everything we do in life must be done by faith. The Bible says whatever is not done by faith is sin (Romans 14:23). Faith is simply this: to receive the Word of God, speak it, do what it says you can do and get what it says you can receive. God promises us in His Word that He heals all our diseases (Psalm 103:3). Therefore, it is our responsibility to refuse to be sick and proclaim that, by His stripes, we are healed (Isaiah 53:5).

God promises that He will bless the righteous with wealth (Deuteronomy 8:18; Proverbs 5:12, 10:22). Therefore, we must refuse to be poor another day in our lives and proclaim that we are plenteous in goods, our storehouses are blessed, our land is blessed, our children are blessed, and our jobs are blessed (Deuteronomy 28:1-14).

God promises He will answer us if we ask Him anything in His name (John 14:14). So, we must pray according to His will and believe we receive whatever we ask for in prayer (Mark 11:24), all according to the Word of God.

When we receive God's Word for our lives and speak it out of our mouths, we are releasing the will of God into our lives. As a man thinks in his heart, so is he (Proverbs 23:7). From the abundance of the heart, the mouth speaks (Luke 6:24).

When we live, speaking by faith, we cause our circumstances to change, just as God caused light to be on the earth when there was only darkness (Genesis 1:3). Whenever we speak by faith, we exercise our God-given authority to change our lives and those around us (John 1:12). We have the ability to be what God wants us to be and do what God wants us to do, all by faith. Begin pleasing God by exercising your faith today (Hebrews 11:6)!

<u>**Mark 11:23**</u> – For verily I say unto you, that whosoever shall say unto this mountain, Be thou removed, and be thou cast into the sea; and shall not doubt in his heart, but shall believe that those things which he saith shall come to pass; he shall have whatsoever he saith.

CP's Signature _____ Date _____

Part 2:
Wisdom & Understanding

Chapter 5:
Wisdom, Prosperity & Decision Making

Prosperity

Deuteronomy 8:18 – But you shall remember the LORD thy God, for it is He who is giving you power to make wealth, that He may confirm His covenant which He swore to your fathers, as it is this day. (NASB)

CP's Signature _____ Date _____

Wisdom

Proverbs 4:7 – Wisdom is the principal thing; therefore, get wisdom: and with all thy getting get understanding.

Proverbs 9:10 – The fear of the LORD is the beginning of wisdom: and the knowledge of the Holy is understanding.

The "fear of the LORD" is not to be in terror or dread, as we use the word today (Proverbs 9:10); rather, this fear is the attitude of refusing to live your life any other way than according to the Word of God (2 Corinthians 7:1); an attitude stemming from a heart to please the LORD in everything we do (Acts 2:43, 9:31); an attitude or way of thinking the Bible says is the beginning of wisdom (Proverbs 9:10).

CP's Signature _____ Date _____

Decision Making

It is often difficult to make decisions. What college should I attend? What church should I join? Am I ready to get married? Which job offer should I accept? To which school should I send my children or should I home school? Should I refinance or should I wait for rates to drop? You get the idea!

It seems as if there are so many important decisions to be made in life that can make or break us (and this is true). How do we decide if there is more than one good choice? We are all faced with these questions and dilemmas, but God has the answer and has provided us with His Word as a roadmap for our decisions. He has promised to order our steps (Psalm 37:23-24).

Whenever you are faced with a tough decision or situation in your life, meditate and **DO** what these Scriptures say, and the Lord will direct your paths (Proverbs 3:5-6).

Whenever we make a decision, it is God's will that we seek His counsel. In addition to seeking counsel from His Word, God has put into each of His children's lives godly men and women who are able to give us sound wisdom, understanding and insight into any situation that may arise in our lives. These counselors include pastors, elders, godly parents and family, and God-fearing friends. It is our responsibility, according to the Word of God, to seek out and heed to these counselors when making decisions in our lives.

Proverbs 13:16 – Every prudent man dealeth with knowledge: but a fool layeth open his folly.

Proverbs 15:22 – Without counsel, purposes are disappointed: but in the multitude of counselors they are established.

Proverbs 18:13 – He that answereth a matter before he heareth it, it is folly and shame unto him.

Proverbs 20:18 – Every purpose is established by counsel: and with good advice make war.

CP's Signature _____ Date _____

The Blessing of Prosperity (Part 1)

Deuteronomy 28:6 – Blessed shalt thou be when thou comest in, and blessed shalt thou be when thou goest out.

Deuteronomy 28:8 – The LORD shall command the blessing upon thee in thy storehouses, and in all that thou settest thine hand unto; and He shall bless thee in the land which the LORD thy God giveth thee.

Psalm 1:3 – And he shall be like a tree planted by the rivers of water, that bringeth forth his fruit in season; his leaf also shall not wither; and whatsoever he doeth shall prosper.

CP's Signature _____ Date _____

Giving and Receiving

One of the most fundamental principles of the Kingdom of God is that of giving and receiving or seedtime and harvest. God promises that we will always receive just as much as we give to others (Luke 6:38). God gave His own Son and received billions of sons in return. He has promised, as long as the earth remains, we will reap a harvest if we are willing to sow (Genesis 8:22; Galatians 6:9).

Malachi 3:10 – Bring ye all the tithes into the storehouse, that there may be meat in Mine house, and prove Me now herewith, saith the LORD of hosts, if I will not open you the windows of heaven, and pour you out a blessing, that there shall not be room enough to receive it.

John 3:16 – For God so loved the world, that He gave His only begotten Son, that whosoever believeth in Him should not perish, but have everlasting life.

Luke 6:38 – Give, and it shall be given unto you; good measure, pressed down, and shaken together, and running over, shall men give into your bosom. For with the same measure that ye mete withal it shall be measured to you again.

2 Corinthians 9:6 – But this I say, He which soweth sparingly shall reap also sparingly; and he which soweth bountifully shall reap also bountifully.

Galatians 6:7 – Be not deceived; God is not mocked: for whatsoever a man soweth, that shall he also reap.

CP's Signature _____ Date _____

Getting Wisdom

Proverbs 4:5 – Get wisdom, get understanding: forget it not; neither decline from the words of my mouth.

James 1:5 – If any of you lacks wisdom, he should ask God, who gives generously to all without finding fault, and it will be given to him. (NIV)

1 John 5:14,15 – And this is the confidence that we have in Him, that, if we ask any thing according to His will, He heareth us: and if we know that He hear us, whatsoever we ask, we know that we have the petitions that we desired of Him.

CP's Signature _____ Date _____

The Blessing of Prosperity (Part 2)

Psalm 5:12 – For Thou, LORD, wilt bless the righteous; with favor wilt Thou compass him as with a shield.

Proverbs 10:22 – The blessing of the LORD, it maketh rich, and He addeth no sorrow with it.

3 John 2 – Beloved, I wish above all things that thou mayest prosper and be in health, even as thy soul prospereth.

CP's Signature _____ Date _____

Chapter 6:
Courtship, Marriage & Dating

Dating & Courtship

Under the Old Covenant, the people of God were not supposed to marry or have relationships with foreigners. God made this commandment, so His people would not make covenant relationships with people who did not worship the True and Living God. He knew, if His people began to marry and make covenants with other peoples, they would fall into sin and pick up all kinds of evil practices from these people: such as idol worship, adultery, fornication, witchcraft and prostitution.

And this is eventually what happened to some of God's people, because they did not heed His Word. God knows that bad company corrupts good morals and you will eventually become like those with whom you have intimate relationships.

Under the New Covenant of Grace and Mercy, God no longer requires us to only marry those who are of the same race or denomination. However, one thing is still the same, we should not marry someone who does not worship the True and Living God, Jesus Christ.

The Word of God clearly instructs us not to be in any kind of covenant relationship (Marriage, Dating, Friendships, Business Partners, etc.) with unbelievers. Why, you ask? For the same basic reason, because God does not want us to pick up the sinful habits of the world and fall into sin (read 2 Corinthians 6:14).

In my lifetime, I have seen and warned many Christian men and women (young and old, friends and family, I might add) that they should get out of their dating relationship or engagement with someone who is not saved and is not seeking every day to please God by faith. Many of them claimed that they were doing nothing wrong, that God would bless them anyway, and that the unbeliever loved them and genuinely cared for them. Often, when I asked them if their significant other is even saved, they often replied, "I think they are."

Listen to me carefully. IT IS NOT GOD'S WILL for any of His children to get into covenant relationship with an unsaved or unbelieving person, no matter how beautiful, handsome, rich, smooth talking, religious, deep, exotic, intelligent, or needy and pitiful. Did I tell you that NONE of the Christian people who I have warned to get out of a relationship with an unbelieving mate are in a successful relationship with that person today? They are either heartbroken, divorced, unfulfilled or trapped in an ungodly relationship that God did not intend.

On the other hand, when we choose God's will for our lives and allow Him to show us the godly man or woman that He desires for us, we are on the road to success. My life with my wife Tiffany seems to get better and better every day because we are both diligently seeking out God's will for our lives and discover how we can love each other more as Christ loved us.

I am not saying that we do not have trials, because we certainly have our fair share. I am simply saying that I have a smile on my face now as I testify to you of the tremendous joy I have as I think about the love God has given my wife and I through Christ Jesus, and everything else just seems small and menial in comparison.

Make a decision today to be in covenant relationship with God and to choose an anointed, believing, respectful, God-pleasing, God-fearing man or woman of God to be your mate and you shall be abundantly rewarded.

Proverbs 18:22 – Whoso findeth a wife findeth a good thing, and obtaineth favor of the LORD.

2 Corinthians 6:14 – Be ye not unequally yoked together with unbelievers: for what fellowship hath righteousness with unrighteousness, and what communion hath light with darkness?

CP's Signature _____ Date _____

Unity and Oneness

Genesis 2:18 – And the LORD God said, It is not good that the man should be alone; I will make him a help meet for him.

Genesis 2:24 – Therefore shall a man leave his father and his mother, and shall cleave unto his wife: and they shall be one flesh.

CP's Signature _____ Date _____

The Power of Agreement

God has ordained marriage to establish the power of agreement. When two people agree, there is nothing they cannot accomplish. The Word says one can chase a thousand and two can put ten thousand to flight (Deuteronomy 32:30). When a man and woman come into agreement with the Word of God, they have supernatural power at their fingertips. Ecclesiastes 4:12 says: "... *a threefold cord is not quickly broken."* In order to become more effective for God, we must make a decision to come into agreement with our loved ones.

The adversary loves to cause division, strife, jealousy and envy in our homes and in our lives, because he knows that this hinders our ability to walk in the power of agreement. When we agree "according to the Word," the Lord promises to always be in the midst of us (Matthew 18:20). Make a decision to agree about one thing with your significant other. Pray and believe God about it every day according to the Word of God and watch God work miracles on your behalf.

<u>Amos 3:3</u> – Can two walk together, except they be agreed?

<u>Matthew 18:19</u> – Again I say unto you, that if two of you shall agree on earth as touching any thing that they shall ask, it shall be done for them of My Father which is in heaven.

<u>Philippians 2:2</u> – Fulfill ye My joy, that ye be like-minded, having the same love, being of one accord, of one mind.

CP's Signature _____ Date _____

<u>Settling Disputes</u>

<u>Proverbs 18:13</u> – He that answereth a matter before he heareth it, it is folly and shame unto him.

<u>Proverbs 29:11</u> – A fool uttereth all his mind: but a wise man keepeth it in till afterward.

<u>Proverbs 18:2</u> – Fools find no pleasure in understanding but delight in airing their own opinions. (NIV)

<u>Romans 14:16</u> – Let not then your good be evil spoken of.

CP's Signature _____ Date _____

So Right, Yet So Wrong!

Did you know that your point of view in an argument or disagreement can be completely right, yet you can still be wrong? (Can I get an "Amen," husbands?) Whatever is not done or said in love is still wrong in the sight of God. Though making a good point in an argument may temporarily make us feel good and shut the mouths of our spouse, family member or even our enemy, it does not always glorify God or help the other person.

The Word teaches us to do whatever leads to peace and mutual edification (Romans 14:19). This may mean putting aside our point of view until another time, so that we might build up our brother or sister in Christ.

Romans 14:19 – Let us therefore make every effort to do what leads to peace and to mutual edification. (NIV)

Ephesians 4:26-27 – Be ye angry, and sin not: let not the sun go down upon your wrath: neither give place to the devil.

Ephesians 5:21 – Submitting yourselves one to another in the fear of God.

CP's Signature _____ Date _____

Order in the Home

Ephesians 5:22 – Wives, submit yourselves unto your own husbands, as unto the Lord.

Ephesians 5:23 – For the husband is the head of the wife, even as Christ is the head of the Church: and He is the savior of the body.

CP's Signature _____ Date _____

The Role of a Husband

<u>John 15:1-2</u> – I am the true vine, and my Father is the husbandman. Every branch in Me that beareth not fruit, He taketh away: and every branch that beareth fruit, He purgeth it, that it may bring forth more fruit.

<u>Ephesians 5:25-26</u> – Husbands, love your wives, even as Christ also loved the Church, and gave Himself for it; that He might sanctify and cleanse it with the washing of water by the Word.

<u>Ephesians 5:27</u> – That He might present it to Himself a glorious Church, not having spot, or wrinkle, or any such thing; but that it should be holy and without blemish.

<u>Ephesians 5:28</u> – So ought men to love their wives as their own bodies. He that loveth his wife loveth himself.

CP's Signature _____ Date _____

The Role of the Wife

<u>Proverbs 14:1</u> – Every wise woman buildeth her house: but the foolish plucketh it down with her hands.

<u>Proverbs 19:14</u> – House and riches are the inheritance of fathers: and a prudent wife is from the LORD.

<u>Proverbs 31:30</u> – Charm is deceptive, and beauty is fleeting; but a woman who fears the LORD is to be praised. (NIV)

CP's Signature _____ Date _____

Love

I believe in love at first sight. From the first day I met my wife, I knew that I loved her. How you ask? Good Question! The Bible says that God is Love (1 John 4:8). It also says that God is the Word (John 1:1). Because of this, you can always know whether someone has God living on the inside of them, by listening to the Word (or lack of it) that comes out of their mouths. For out of the abundance of the heart, the mouth speaks (Luke 6:45).

When I first met my wife, Tiffany, I knew that I loved her because she had God exuding out of her. I could see in her the same love for God that I had in me. So, I immediately knew that I loved her.

I believe that God meant every man to find a wife in this way. A man and woman are to first know and dwell in God separately. Then, they will be able to supernaturally recognize and fall in love with the unique love for God burning on the inside of one another, together.

John 15:12 – This is my commandment, that ye love one another, as I have loved you.

Romans 8:28 – And we know that all things work together for good to them that love God, to them who are the called according to His purpose.

1 John 4:8 – He that loveth not, knoweth not God; for God is Love.

1 John 4:16 – And we have known and believed the love that God hath to us. God is Love; and he that dwelleth in love dwelleth in God, and God in him.

CP's Signature _____ Date _____

Chapter 7:
Strength, Power &
the Righteousness of God

God is Our Strength

Oftentimes, as we go throughout life, we begin to be wearied by the problems we face from day to day. It is easy to become stressed by the daily routine of work, school, housekeeping and paying bills, just to name a few. It is during these times, we need strength to continue on and not be discouraged by the things that life throws at us.

Instead of trying in our own strength to endure, the Word instructs us to make the Lord our strength. When we allow God to be our strength, we are able to overcome any obstacle that gets in our way. The Bible says it this way, *"If God be for us, who can be against us?"* (Romans 8:31). With God as our strength, there is nothing we cannot do.

Psalm 18:2 – The LORD is my rock, and my fortress, and my deliverer; my God, my strength, in whom I will trust; my buckler, and the horn of my salvation, and my high tower.

Psalm 27:1 – The LORD is my light and my salvation; whom shall I fear? The LORD is the strength of my life; of whom shall I be afraid?

Philippians 4:13 – I can do all things through Christ which strengtheneth me.

CP's Signature _____ Date _____

Power

Deuteronomy 8:18 – But you shall remember the LORD your God, for it is He who is giving you power to make wealth, that He may confirm His covenant which He swore to your fathers, as it is this day. (NAS)

John 1:12 – But as many as received Him, to them gave He power to become the sons of God, even to them that believe on His name.

Ephesians 3:20 – Now unto Him that is able to do exceeding abundantly above all that we ask or think, according to the power that worketh in us.

 2 Timothy 1:7 – For God hath not given us the spirit of fear; but of power, and of love, and of a sound mind.

1 John 4:4 – Ye are of God, little children, and have overcome them: because greater is He that is in you, than he that is in the world.

CP's Signature _____ Date _____

Who are the Righteous?

Often, when teaching on the subject of righteousness to Christians, I ask everyone who is righteous to please raise their hand. I am never surprised to see that almost no one is willing to raise their hand, even after being taught about righteousness. The Bible says that Christ, who was without sin, died for us, so that we might become the righteousness of God (2 Corinthians 5:21).

It is not optional. Just as we are saved when we believe in Jesus, at the same moment, we are also made the righteousness of God. What does this mean? It means, when we get saved, we are instantly put in "right-standing" with God through the blood of Jesus.

To be righteous means that we now have a right to everything Jesus possessed when He was on earth (John 16:15). As the righteousness of God, we have:

- a right to be healed (Isaiah 53:4-5),
- a right to have wisdom (1 Corinthians 2:7),
- a right to be wealthy (Deuteronomy 8:18),
- a right to have our children blessed (Isaiah 54:13),
- a right to be victorious (Romans 8:37),
- and so much more!

The righteous are those who have chosen to live for Christ and to seek first God's way of being right (Matthew 6:33). The righteousness of this world is founded in self-righteousness, but the righteousness of God is founded in Jesus Christ who died for the sins of the world. We did nothing to earn salvation and there is nothing we can do to be made righteous. Because Jesus paid it all, we are the righteousness of God.

Righteousness (Part 1)

Psalm 5:12 – For Thou, LORD, wilt bless the righteous; with favor wilt Thou compass him as with a shield.

Isaiah 54:17 – No weapon that is formed against thee shall prosper; and every tongue that shall rise against thee in judgment, thou shalt condemn. This is the heritage of the servants of the LORD, and their righteousness is of Me, saith the LORD.

Romans 10:9-10 – That if thou shall confess with thy mouth the Lord Jesus, and shalt believe in thine heart that God hath raised Him from the dead, thou shalt be saved. For with the heart man believeth unto righteousness; and with the mouth confession is made unto salvation.

2 Corinthians 5:21 – For He hath made Him to be sin for us, who knew no sin; that we might be made the righteousness of God in Him.

> **Righteousness** – The state of being right or to be in right standing with God (2 Corinthians 5:21); God's way of being right or correct (Romans 3:21); the position of lining-up according to the Word of God (Romans 1:17).

James 5:16 – Confess your faults one to another, and pray one for another, that ye may be healed. The effectual fervent prayer of a righteous man availeth much.

CP's Signature _____ Date _____

Righteousness (Part 2)

Matthew 5:6 – Blessed are they which do hunger and thirst after righteousness: for they shall be filled.

Matthew 6:33 – But seek ye first the Kingdom of God, and His righteousness; and all these things shall be added unto you.

Romans 1:17 – For therein is the righteousness of God revealed from faith to faith: as it is written, the just shall live by faith.

2 Timothy 2:22 – Flee also youthful lusts: but follow righteousness, faith, charity, peace, with them that call on the Lord out of a pure heart.

2 Timothy 3:16 – All Scripture is given by inspiration of God, and is profitable for doctrine, for reproof, for correction, for instruction in righteousness.

Titus 3:5 – Not by works of righteousness which we have done, but according to His mercy He saved us, by the washing of regeneration, and renewing of the Holy Ghost.

CP's Signature _____ Date _____

Part 3:
The Spiritual Kingdom

Chapter 8:
The Manifestations of the Holy Spirit

<u>The Promise of the Spirit</u>

The Holy Spirit is our guide for victorious living. Jesus promised, if He did not leave, the Holy Spirit could not come (John 16:7). The Holy Spirit is our life blood. We are to be filled with the Holy Ghost (Ephesians 5:18). He is our connection to the Father in Heaven.

Without the Spirit of God, we would have no way of truly knowing our Father is real because He lives so far away in heaven. The Holy Spirit testifies with our spirit that we are God's children (Romans 8:16). Without His Spirit, we would be orphans in the land (John 14:18).

<u>John 15:26</u> – But when the Comforter is come, whom I will send unto you from the Father, even the Spirit of truth, which proceedeth from the Father, He will testify of Me.

<u>John 16:13</u> – Howbeit, when He, the Spirit of truth, is come, He will guide you into all truth: for He shall not speak of Himself; but whatsoever He shall hear, that shall He speak: and He will show you things to come.

CP's Signature _____ Date _____

<u>God is a Spirit</u>

<u>John 4:24</u> – God is a Spirit: and they that worship Him must worship Him in spirit and in truth.

2 Corinthians 3:17 – Now the Lord is that Spirit: and where the Spirit of the Lord is, there is liberty.

CP's Signature _____ Date _____

The Nine Gifts of the Spirit

But the manifestation of the Spirit is given to every man to profit withal. For to one is given by the Spirit, the word of wisdom; to another, the word of knowledge by the same Spirit; To another, faith by the same Spirit; to another, the gifts of healing by the same Spirit; To another, the working of miracles; to another, prophecy; to another, discerning of spirits; to another, divers kinds of tongues; to another, the interpretation of tongues: but all these worketh that one and the selfsame Spirit, dividing to every man severally as He will. (1 Corinthians 12:7-11)

These special endowments are what the Scriptures call the nine manifestations or gifts of the Holy Spirit. These are not all the gifts, but they represent those available to every believer. When we receive the Holy Spirit, we receive these nine gifts. The question is not, "How many of these gifts do I possess?" The question is, "Do you have the Holy Spirit?"

Either, you have the Holy Ghost or you do not. The gifts belong to Him, not you and me. This is why they are called the manifestation of the Spirit. They are not your manifestations or my manifestations. (See page 141.)

If you have the Holy Ghost, then you have all nine gifts on the inside of you. If you do not have the Holy Ghost, then you have zero (0) gifts within you. There is no Half-Holy Spirit or Quarter-Holy Spirit. There is no need to discover if you have four or five gifts. All nine gifts are on the inside of you if you are born again. Like any gift, these manifestations need only to be opened and used by the believer. If we do not open them, then they will not manifest. Simple. Where the Spirit of the Lord is, there is liberty (2 Corinthians 3:17).

1) Word of Wisdom
2) Word of Knowledge
3) Faith
4) Gifts of Healing
5) Working of Miracles
6) Prophecy
7) Discerning of Spirits
8) Divers Kinds of Tongues
9) Interpretation of Tongues

Only memorize the names of the Nine Gifts of the Spirit.

CP's Signature _____ Date _____

The Nine Fruit of the Spirit

But the fruit of the Spirit is love, joy, peace, longsuffering, gentleness, goodness, faith, meekness, temperance: against such there is no law. (Galatians 5:22-23)

God is glorified when we bear much fruit (John 15:8). Fruit implies that a seed must be planted, watered, grown and harvested. The fruit of the Spirit follow this same spiritual principle of sowing and reaping. Unlike the nine gifts of the Spirit, the fruit cannot simply be opened and used. They must be cultivated and grown as a part of a healthy Christian lifestyle. (See page 138.)

It takes some people an entire lifetime to learn to love correctly. Longsuffering (aka patience) is only cultivated through the trying of our faith (James 1:2-4). Meekness (aka humility) is birthed when the Lord resists the pride in our lives (James 4:6; 1 Peter 5:5).

We must learn that Joy is not tied to happiness. Only experience teaches us that true peace goes beyond our understanding (Philippians 4:7), and so forth. We are His true disciples when we bear much fruit.

1) Love
2) Joy
3) Peace
4) Longsuffering
5) Gentleness

6) Goodness
7) Faith
8) Meekness
9) Temperance

Only memorize the names of the Nine Fruit of the Spirit.

CP's Signature _____ Date _____

Don't Deny the Power

Now that we have explored the nine gifts and nine fruit of the Spirit, it is important we operate in the power of the Holy Ghost. We are not to keep His gifts to ourselves, but use them to impact the lives of others for Christ. Jesus promised that He would give us power to affect the world around us through the Spirit of God (Acts 1:8).

His manifestations are to be used with both boldness and humility to show the world that the Kingdom of God is real and relevant. We are not to withhold the authority and power, but rather, to use them to cause His Kingdom to come on earth as it is in Heaven.

Proverbs 3:27 – Withhold not good from them to whom it is due, when it is in the power of thine hand to do it.

Acts 1:8 – But ye shall receive power, after that the Holy Ghost is come upon you: and ye shall be witnesses unto Me both in Jerusalem, and in all Judaea, and in Samaria, and unto the uttermost part of the earth.

2 Timothy 3:5 – Having a form of godliness, but denying the power thereof: from such turn away.

CP's Signature _____ Date _____

Chapter 9:
Prophecy & Tongues

<u>Prophecy is the Key</u>

Jesus promised to send us the Comforter to perpetuate the greatest release of Heaven this planet has ever seen: the pouring out of the Spirit of God on all flesh to prophesy. This outpouring would release a new precedent on the earth to make the Holy Ghost available to God's people across gender, class and racial lines:

> *But this is that which was spoken by the prophet Joel; and it shall come to pass in the last days, saith God, I will pour out of My Spirit upon all flesh: and your sons and your daughters shall prophesy, and your young men shall see visions, and your old men shall dream dreams: and on My servants and on My handmaidens I will pour out in those days of My Spirit; and they shall prophesy: (Acts 2:16-18)*

> *Pursue love, yet desire earnestly spiritual gifts, but especially that you may prophesy. (1 Corinthians 14:1 NASB)*

To prophesy means to forth-tell while under the influence of the Holy Ghost. The gift of prophecy is about receiving revelation from the Father in Heaven for the purpose of building God's people, the Church, both collectively and individually. Jesus planned to build the Church based on revelation from the Father (Matthew 16:15-19).

Tongues & Prophecy

Jesus began making the Holy Spirit available to build the Church using the gifts of tongues and prophecy on the day of Pentecost (Acts 2). The gift of tongues is simply prophesying in a language unknown to the speaker. The gift of tongues was the first gift made available to the Body of Christ when the Father chose to pour out His Spirit on that day. We are commanded to not forbid speaking in tongues (1 Corinthians 14:39).

However, the Scriptures make it clear that the gift of tongues is a means to prophesy (Acts 2:16). In fact, we are told that prophecy is the best of the nine gifts of the Spirit (1 Corinthians 14:1). Prophecy builds or edifies the Church. The gift of tongues edifies (or builds) the individual (1 Corinthians 14:4). It carries the exact same weight as prophecy when the interpretation is given (1 Corinthians 14:5, 13). Both gifts are necessary in the Body of Christ.

1 Corinthians 14:3 – But he that prophesieth speaketh unto men to edification, and exhortation, and comfort.

CP's Signature _____ Date _____

Tongues Only

When we speak in an unknown tongue, we are praying in the Spirit. The gift of tongues allows us to be built up on our most holy faith in the Lord. Faith is necessary to please God with our lives.

There are many practical applications for praying in the Holy Ghost: spiritual warfare, worshipping the Father, receiving revelation, strengthening our weaknesses, etc. The most basic utility of praying in tongues is that we do not know what we are saying, initially. This allows us to pray to the Father without our doubt and unbelief getting in the way of the release of our faith.

It is usually quite surprising to new tongues-talkers that praying is much easier when done in the Spirit. Most believers who learn to pray in tongues realize they can pray much longer in tongues than in their native language.

1 Corinthians 14:2 – For he that speaketh in an unknown tongue speaketh not unto men, but unto God: for no man understandeth him; howbeit in the spirit he speaketh mysteries.

1 Corinthians 14:14 – For if I pray in an unknown tongue, my spirit prayeth, but my understanding is unfruitful.

Jude 1:20 – But ye, beloved, building up yourselves on your most holy faith, praying in the Holy Ghost,

CP's Signature _____ Date _____

The Holy Spirit's Intercession

Romans 8:26 – Likewise, the Spirit also helpeth our infirmities: for we know not what we should pray for as we ought: but the Spirit itself maketh intercession for us with groanings which cannot be uttered.

CP's Signature _____ Date _____

Prophecy Only

Prophecy builds the Church. It is for edification, exhortation and comfort (1 Corinthians 14:3). Edification means to build up. Exhortation means to lift up. Comfort means to help (and is also why the Holy Ghost is called the Helper or Comforter).

We need prophecy to grow and build the Church correctly. It was not just for the Old Testament saints, but is a gift of the New Testament Church. It was meant by Christ to be a pivotal tool to prepare God's people for works of service (Ephesians 4:11-12).

1 Corinthians 14:3 – But he that prophesieth speaketh unto men to edification, and exhortation, and comfort.

1 Corinthians 14:4 – He that speaketh in an unknown tongue edifieth himself; but he that prophesieth edifieth the Church.

CP's Signature _____ Date _____

Dreams & Visions

The gift of prophecy frequently works through dreams and visions. Simply explained, dreams are spiritual, cinematic events we see while we are sleeping. Visions are dreams we receive while we are awake, usually small in time-span. Dreams and visions are the oldest form of heavenly communication on earth. They allow God to get our attention when we are unable to interrupt the communication line (Job 33:14-16).

When we prophesy, it is common for us to see a scene in our mind's eye about the person(s) to whom we are speaking. A vision is usually more literal, making it easier to interpret and speak to the hearer. A dream is usually more symbolic, making it harder to interpret and, therefore, requires more time and prayer to be understood.

<u>**Numbers 12:6**</u> – And He said, Hear now My words: If there be a prophet among you, I the LORD will make Myself known unto him in a vision, and will speak unto him in a dream.

<u>**Acts 2:17**</u> – And it shall come to pass in the last days, saith God, I will pour out of My Spirit upon all flesh: and your sons and your daughters shall prophesy, and your young men shall see visions, and your old men shall dream dreams.

CP's Signature _____ Date _____

Write the Vision

<u>**Habakkuk 2:2**</u> – And the LORD answered me, and said, Write the vision, and make it plain upon tables, that he may run that readeth it.

CP's Signature _____ Date _____

Chapter 10:
Healing & Deliverance

Healing for Our Bodies

One of the central ministries of Christ was the ministry of physical healing. It is God's desire that we remain physically healthy in our bodies and be free from sickness and disease. Jesus healed the man with the withered hand (Luke 6:10). Jesus gave sight to the blind (Matthew 9:29-30). He caused the death and dumb to hear and speak (Mark 9:25).

Jesus told the sick of the palsy to rise up and walk (Luke 5:24). The woman with the issue of blood got healed (Luke 8:44), and many more. When asked if it was the Lord's will to heal, He simply replied, "I will" (Mark 1:41). God's will is for His people to be healed.

We never read in Scripture where Jesus came across someone who wanted to be healed and they did not leave whole. Why? The answer is simple: God "will" heal everyone who believes He "will" do it for them. Jesus said, *"If thou canst believe, all things are possible to him that believeth."* (Mark 9:23) We must choose to only believe this (Luke 8:50), and we will always receive our healing.

<u>Isaiah 53:4</u> – Surely He hath borne our griefs, and carried our sorrows: yet we did esteem Him stricken, smitten of God, and afflicted.

<u>Isaiah 53:5</u> – But He was wounded for our transgressions, He was bruised for our iniquities: the chastisement of our peace was upon Him; and with His stripes we are healed.

CP's Signature _____ Date _____

Through the Laying on of Hands

In the Old Testament, the laying on of hands released blessings from a father to a son. Whenever a man of God wanted to make sure his son would be blessed and prosperous all the days of his life, he would simply lay hands on him and speak all the blessings of God into his son's life.

In the New Testament, God has given us His Holy Spirit and the Father now dwells in us. Because of this, we now have the authority to lay hands on one another as the Father leads us, and to speak forth the blessings of God to heal, forgive sins, impart gifts, bless and live abundant lives as sons of God (2 Timothy 1:6, James 5:14-15).

<u>Mark 16:17-18</u> – And these signs shall follow them that believe; in My name shall they cast out devils; they shall speak with new tongues; they shall take up serpents; and if they drink any deadly thing, it shall not hurt them; they shall lay hands on the sick, and they shall recover.

CP's Signature _____ Date _____

Through Prayer, Faith and Anointing with Oil

<u>James 5:14</u> – Is any sick among you? Let Him call for the elders of the church; and let them pray over him, anointing him with oil in the name of the Lord.

<u>**James 5:15**</u> – And the prayer of faith shall save the sick, and the Lord shall raise him up; and if he have committed sins, they shall be forgiven him.

CP's Signature _____ Date _____

<u>Through Confessing Our Sins and Prayer</u>

<u>**James 5:16**</u> – Confess your faults one to another, and pray one for another, that ye may be healed. The effectual fervent prayer of a righteous man availeth much.

CP's Signature _____ Date _____

<u>The Lord that Heals Us</u>

<u>**Malachi 4:2**</u> – But unto you that fear My name shall the Sun of righteousness arise with healing in His wings; and ye shall go forth, and grow up as calves of the stall.

<u>**Exodus 15:26**</u> – And said, If thou wilt diligently hearken to the voice of the LORD thy God, and wilt do that which is right in His sight, and wilt give ear to His commandments, and keep all His statutes, I will put none of these diseases upon thee, which I have brought upon the Egyptians: for I am the LORD that healeth thee.

CP's Signature _____ Date _____

<u>Prosperity and Health</u>

<u>**3 John 2**</u> – Beloved, I wish above all things that thou mayest prosper and be in health, even as thy soul prospereth.

CP's Signature _____ Date _____

Healing the Land

2 Chronicles 7:14 – If My people, which are called by My name, shall humble themselves, and pray, and seek My face, and turn from their wicked ways; then will I hear from heaven, and will forgive their sin, and will heal their land.

CP's Signature _____ Date _____

The Ministry of Deliverance

The ministry of deliverance represents Spiritual Healing in the Health Care System of the Kingdom of God. Deliverance is needed to set free God's people that are oppressed of the devil. We need healing and deliverance. Deliverance cleans the house while healing fills the house again.

Deliverance removes the kingdom of darkness from our lives while healing fills it with the Kingdom of Light. Jesus preached deliverance to the captives (Luke 4:18). He came to set at liberty them that are bruised. Whom the Son sets free is free indeed.

Isaiah 49:9a – That thou mayest say to the prisoners, go forth; to them that are in darkness, shew yourselves.

CP's Signature _____ Date _____

Healing the Brokenhearted

Deliverance ministry is to heal the brokenhearted. God once sent me to a church to simply tell His people that he was going to heal the brokenhearted. This church was filled with people with lives bruised and scarred by past experiences and present disappointments.

Our hearts are broken by unkept promises our friends and loved ones have made to us. Our hearts are broken when we do not receive the things for which we have been dreaming for many years.

Our children break our hearts when they disobey us. We are left wounded and rejected by those who have told us we will never be successful and we will never amount to anything. Our hearts are broken when those we call friends leave us and forsake us.

Jesus said He came to heal the brokenhearted. To heal means to mend, set into place and restore something to its original state of effectiveness. This means that God can pick up the broken pieces of our lives and mend our hearts and minds so that there will be nothing missing and nothing broken. He can restore everything that the devil has stolen from us and make our lives as if they were never broken.

He will keep every promise He has made to us. He will never leave us or forsake us.

Psalm 147:3 – He healeth the broken in heart, and bindeth up their wounds.

Luke 4:18 – The Spirit of the Lord is upon me, because He hath anointed me to preach the gospel to the poor; He hath sent me to heal the brokenhearted, to preach deliverance to the captives, and recovering of sight to the blind, to set at liberty them that are bruised.

CP's Signature _____ Date _____

Healing the Oppressed

Acts 10:38 – How God anointed Jesus of Nazareth with the Holy Ghost and with power: who went about doing good, and healing all that were oppressed of the devil; for God was with Him.

CP's Signature _____ Date _____

Our Healing Mandate

John 14:12 – Verily, verily, I say unto you, He that believeth on Me, the works that I do shall he do also; and greater works than these shall he do; because I go unto My Father.

Mark 16:17-18 – And these signs shall follow them that believe; in My name shall they cast out devils; they shall speak with new tongues; they shall take up serpents; and if they drink any deadly thing, it shall not hurt them; they shall lay hands on the sick, and they shall recover.

CP's Signature _____ Date _____

Our Healing & Deliverance Authority

Luke 10:19 – Behold, I give unto you power to tread on serpents and scorpions, and over all the power of the enemy: and nothing shall by any means hurt you.

Acts 1:8 – But ye shall receive power, after that the Holy Ghost is come upon you: and ye shall be witnesses unto Me both in Jerusalem, and in all Judaea, and in Samaria, and unto the uttermost part of the earth.

CP's Signature _____ Date _____

Through the Laying on of Hands (Part 2)

Proverbs 3:27 – Withhold not good from them to whom it is due, when it is in the power of thine hand to do it.

Mark 16:17-18 – And these signs shall follow them that believe; in My name shall they cast out devils; they shall speak with new tongues; they shall take up serpents; and if they drink any deadly thing, it shall not hurt them; they shall lay hands on the sick, and they shall recover.

CP's Signature _____ Date _____

The Kingdom Healthcare Plan

Psalm 103:1 – Bless the LORD, O my soul: and all that is within me, bless His holy name.

Psalm 103:2 – Bless the LORD, O my soul, and forget not all His benefits.

Psalm 103:3 – Who forgiveth all thine iniquities; who healeth all thy diseases.

CP's Signature _____ Date _____

Chapter 11:
Angels & the Flames of Fire

One of the greatest mysteries in the Kingdom of God is the operation of the oldest clandestine organization in the universe, the Heavenly Host. The Heavenly Host is the Secret Service of Heaven and the military arm of the Kingdom of God. Quite often in the Old Testament, we hear the Scriptures refer to God as the LORD of Hosts. This is talking about God being the Commander of the armies.

They are an innumerable company of angels sent to bring the Lord's will to pass (Hebrews 12:22).

Psalm 103:20 – Bless the LORD, ye His angels, that excel in strength, that do His commandments, hearkening unto the voice of His Word.

Psalm 103:21 Bless ye the LORD, all ye His hosts; ye ministers of His, that do His pleasure.

CP's Signature _____ Date _____

The Flames of Fire

The most hidden assignment of His angels is that they are assigned to minister for every born again believer. They are assigned and sent to serve those who shall inherit salvation (Hebrews 1:14). An angel was assigned to Moses to help him deliver the children of Israel from Egypt. The Angel of the Lord did signs, wonders and miracles on Moses' behalf (Acts 7:35). That angel showed up as a flame of fire in the burning bush (Acts 7:30).

An angel was assigned to Jacob to protect him and secure his legacy as the Father of Israel (Genesis 48:16). The angels are assigned to us today to help us do the works of Christ (Hebrews 2:1-4). They are the reason that signs will follow those who believe in His name (Mark 16:17-18). We literally have an angel following us everywhere we go to help His Word come to pass.

Hebrews 1:7 – And of the angels He saith, Who maketh His angels spirits, and His ministers a flame of fire.

Hebrews 1:14 – Are they not all ministering spirits, sent forth to minister for them who shall be heirs of salvation?

CP's Signature _____ Date _____

<u>Angelic Protection</u>

Psalm 91:11 – For He shall give His angels charge over thee, to keep thee in all thy ways.

Matthew 18:10 – Take heed that ye despise not one of these little ones; for I say unto you, that in heaven their angels do always behold the face of My Father which is in heaven.

CP's Signature _____ Date _____

Chapter 12:
Spiritual Warfare

The Whole Armor of God

Christ has given the Church dominion on earth as it is in Heaven. We are to subdue the earth and cause His Kingdom to come and His will to be done. We are to exercise our authority over the enemy. We are called to make His enemies His footstool (Psalm 110:1-2; Romans 16:20). Our King will return when all things have been put under His feet (Acts, 2:19-21; Hebrews 2:8).

To win, we must be prepared for the battle. God has given us the necessary armor. We are commanded to put on the whole armor of God (Ephesians 6:11). Our armor is designed to stand against the wiles of the devil. It addresses every area of spiritual warfare (Ephesians 6:14-18):

1) Loins girt with **Truth**
2) Breastplate of **Righteousness**
3) Feet shod with the preparation of the Gospel of **Peace**
4) Shield of **Faith** to quench the fiery darts of the wicked
5) Helmet of **Salvation**
6) Sword of the Spirit, the **Word of God** to pray in the Spirit

Only memorize the six parts of the Armor of God.

CP's Signature _____ Date _____

The Weapons of Our Warfare

The whole armor of God is a necessity. The Scriptures tell us these weapons of our warfare are not of this world (2 Corinthians 10:4). We have been given otherworldly weapons to defeat the enemy. Our weapons are designed to pull down thoughts and imaginations that have been deeply established by the enemy. These deeply rooted thoughts are called strongholds.

The enemy operates by affecting the mind so that he can control the entire person (Proverbs 23:7). He that has control of the mind has control of the whole body to affect a person's desires, will and motivations. Strongholds open up the body to all kinds of sicknesses and diseases, both psychological and physiological.

Our weapons are given to us to transcend the limitations of the physical realm; they allow us to get to the source of the enemy's schemes against us.

2 Corinthians 10:3 – For though we walk in the flesh, we do not war after the flesh.

2 Corinthians 10:4 – (For the weapons of our warfare are not carnal, but mighty through God to the pulling down of strong holds;)

2 Corinthians 10:5 – Casting down imaginations, and every high thing that exalteth itself against the knowledge of God, and bringing into captivity every thought to the obedience of Christ.

CP's Signature _____ Date _____

Christ's Position of Power (Part 1)

Ephesians 1:20 – Which He wrought in Christ, when He raised Him from the dead, and set Him at His own right hand in the heavenly places,

Ephesians 1:21 – Far above all principality, and power, and might, and dominion, and every name that is named, not only in this world, but also in that which is to come.

CP's Signature _____ Date _____

Christ's Position of Power (Part 2)

Psalm 110:1 – The LORD said unto my Lord, Sit Thou at My right hand, until I make Thine enemies Thy footstool.

Psalm 110:2 – The LORD shall send the rod of Thy strength out of Zion: rule Thou in the midst of Thine enemies.

CP's Signature _____ Date _____

Our Authority in Christ

Luke 10:19 – Behold, I give unto you power to tread on serpents and scorpions, and over all the power of the enemy: and nothing shall by any means hurt you.

CP's Signature _____ Date _____

Our Position in Christ

Ephesians 1:3 – Blessed be the God and Father of our Lord Jesus Christ, who hath blessed us with all spiritual blessings in heavenly places in Christ.

CP's Signature _____ Date _____

Warfare Protection (Part 1)

Deuteronomy 28:7 – The LORD shall cause thine enemies that rise up against thee to be smitten before thy face: they shall come out against thee one way, and flee before thee seven ways.

Isaiah 54:17 – No weapon that is formed against thee shall prosper; and every tongue that shall rise against thee in judgment Thou shalt condemn. This is the heritage of the servants of the LORD, and their righteousness is of Me, saith the LORD.

CP's Signature _____ Date _____

Warfare Protection (Part 2)

Psalm 91:7 – A thousand shall fall at thy side, and ten thousand at thy right hand; but it shall not come nigh thee.

Psalm 91:10 – There shall no evil befall thee, neither shall any plague come nigh thy dwelling.

Luke 10:19 – Behold, I give unto you power to tread on serpents and scorpions, and over all the power of the enemy: and nothing shall by any means hurt you.

CP's Signature _____ Date _____

Chapter 13:
The 4-Fold Ministry

Jesus Christ, the King of kings, is the Head of the Church (Ephesian 1:22; Colossians 1:18). The Church, the *Ecclesia*, is the many membered body of believers assigned to rule with Christ on earth as it is in Heaven. The Church is the legislative body of the Kingdom of God. Christ intended for His Church to be a government, not a religious organization; for the Scriptures say the government shall be upon His shoulders (Isaiah 9:6).

Like any kingdom government, the Kingdom of God is also ruled by a King who has appointed officers to help rule His Kingdom. These appointed officials in a kingdom are called ministers. These ministers have administrations that are government ordained departments and that keep the government healthy and responsible. For example, the United Kingdom of Great Britain is led by a Prime Minister who has a Minister of Defense, a Minister of Education, etc.

These offices are equivalent to the Secretary of Defense and the Secretary of Education in our U.S. government. Jesus Christ, the King, has appointed in the government of His Kingdom Church some to be apostles, prophets, evangelists, and pastor-teachers (Ephesians 4:11). These offices represent the four grace Gifts of Christ (see page 140), also called the 4-Fold ministry (Ephesians 4:7). [Note: Some also call this the 5-fold ministry. I teach that it is the 4-fold ministry because I believe that it is more accurate that Pastor and Teacher is one gift and not two separate gifts, in context.]

All of these offices are a part of the administration of Jesus Christ (1 Corinthians 12:5, 28; Ephesians 4:7-12). They are appointed to help Jesus build the Church (Matthew 16:18; Ephesians 4:12) and run the Kingdom of God.

Ephesians 4:11 – And He gave some, apostles; and some, prophets; and some, evangelists; and some, pastors and teachers.

Ephesians 4:12 – For the perfecting of the saints, for the work of the ministry, for the edifying of the Body of Christ.

CP's Signature _____ Date _____

Building On The Foundation

Jesus wanted to build His Church. The word *build* is the same word *edify* in the New Testament. Edify is the root of the word *edifice* which means *building* or structure. When Jesus said He wanted to build His Church (Matthew 16:18), He was saying He wanted to edify His Church. The Church receives edification through the Holy Spirit's gift of prophecy by the revelation that He gives the Body of Christ (1 Corinthians 14:3).

Consequently, Jesus created the offices of apostle and prophet to be the primary gifts that prophesy and release revelation to the Body of Christ (Ephesians 3:3-5). This explains why the Scriptures say the apostles and prophets are the foundation of the Church, they are primarily responsible to edify or build it (Ephesians 2:20, 4:12).

1 Corinthians 3:11 – For other foundation can no man lay than that is laid, which is Jesus Christ.

1 Corinthians 14:3 – But he that prophesieth speaketh unto men to edification, and exhortation, and comfort.

Ephesians 2:20 – And are built upon the foundation of the apostles and prophets, Jesus Christ Himself being the Chief Corner Stone.

Ephesians 3:5 – Which in other ages was not made known unto the sons of men, as it is now revealed unto His holy apostles and prophets by the Spirit.

CP's Signature _____ Date _____

Revelation through the Prophets

Amos 3:7 – Surely the Lord GOD will do nothing, but He revealeth His secret unto His servants the prophets.

CP's Signature _____ Date _____

The Work of the Evangelist

Evangelists are the immigration officers of the Kingdom of God. They are responsible to naturalize those outside the Kingdom that desire to become citizens. Evangelists are primarily concerned with saving souls and getting souls that are already saved to be more Kingdom-minded. They lead God's people to be born again (John 3:3).

An evangelist desires that no one in or outside the Kingdom is lost. They want the lost to be found. They believe every person deserves another chance to get into the Kingdom of God. The evangelist represents the true heart of the Father that none should perish (2 Peter 3:9).

Romans 10:15 – And how shall they preach, except they be sent? as it is written, How beautiful are the feet of them that preach the gospel of peace, and bring glad tidings of good things!

2 Timothy 4:5 – But watch thou in all things, endure afflictions, do the work of an evangelist, make full proof of thy ministry.

CP's Signature _____ Date _____

Pastors According to God's Heart

The word *pastor* is the same word *shepherd* in the Bible. A spiritual shepherd is someone that leads and feeds the flock of God by the Word of God. The pastor specifically feeds the flock of God with knowledge and understanding (Jeremiah 3:15), creating the gift of pastor and teacher or pastor-teacher.

With this understanding we know that the pastor is a shepherd that leads and feeds the flock of God through teaching the Word of God. Their goal is to make sure that God's people understand the Scriptures and do not perish because of a lack of knowledge (Hosea 4:6). These are the kinds of shepherds that lead after God's own heart.

Psalm 23:1 – The LORD is my Shepherd; I shall not want.

Psalm 23:2 – He maketh me to lie down in green pastures: He leadeth me beside the still waters.

Psalm 23:3 – He restoreth my soul: He leadeth me in the paths of righteousness for His name's sake.

Jeremiah 3:15 – And I will give you pastors according to Mine heart, which shall feed you with knowledge and understanding.

CP's Signature _____ Date _____

The Shepherd of the Sheep

<u>John 10:2</u> – But he that entereth in by the door is the shepherd of the sheep.

<u>John 10:3</u> – To him the porter openeth; and the sheep hear his voice: and he calleth his own sheep by name, and leadeth them out.

CP's Signature _____ Date _____

The Order of the Church

<u>**1 Corinthians 12:28**</u> – And God hath set some in the church, first apostles, secondarily prophets, thirdly teachers, after that miracles, then gifts of healings, helps, governments, diversities of tongues.

CP's Signature _____ Date _____

Part 4:
Rooted & Grounded

Chapter 14:
The Psalms

The book of Psalms is among the most read books of the Bible. Most everyone is familiar with the 23rd Psalm.

A friend of mine once preached an awesome message about how we all loved the Psalms and the importance of the very first Psalm. In his sermon, he recited from memory, as he preached, many of the Psalms in their entirety (at least that is how it seemed). While he went through each of our favorite Psalms, the crowd went wild. To this day, I do not know what stopped us all from reaching up into the pulpit and grabbing him while he was preaching, he was preaching so well!

But this is how wonderful the Psalms have become to us who have taken the time to meditate on them. The Psalms, largely written by King David, speak to us about every area of our lives. It is through the Psalms that we learn that the Lord is our Shepherd (Psalm 23), that His Word is a lamp to our feet and a light unto our path (Psalm 119:105), that God is our light and our salvation (Psalm 27), that He will never leave or forsake us (Psalm 37:25). What would we do without the Psalms?

As you go through this last chapter, please take the time meditate on the Word of God and the Psalms will quickly change your life forever. It will be easy to see why we all love the Psalms.

Psalm 1

1   Blessed is the man that walketh not in the counsel of the ungodly, nor standeth in the way of sinners, nor sitteth in the seat of the scornful.

2   But his delight is in the law of the LORD; and in His law doth he meditate day and night.

3   And he shall be like a tree planted by the rivers of water, that bringeth forth his fruit in his season; his leaf also shall not wither; and whatsoever he doeth shall prosper.

4   The ungodly are not so: but are like the chaff which the wind driveth away.

5   Therefore the ungodly shall not stand in the judgment, nor sinners in the congregation of the righteous.

6   For the LORD knoweth the way of the righteous: but the way of the ungodly shall perish.

CP's Signature _____ Date _____

Psalm 23

1   The LORD is my Shepherd; I shall not want.

2   He maketh me to lie down in green pastures: He leadeth me beside the still waters.

3   He restoreth my soul: He leadeth me in the paths of righteousness for His name's sake.

4   Yea, though I walk through the valley of the shadow of death, I will fear no evil: for Thou art with me; Thy rod and Thy staff they comfort me.

5   Thou preparest a table before me in the presence of mine enemies: Thou anointest my head with oil; my cup runneth over.

6   Surely goodness and mercy shall follow me all the days of my life: and I will dwell in the house of the LORD forever.

CP's Signature _____ Date _____

Psalm 37:1-6

1   Fret not thyself because of evildoers, neither be thou envious against the workers of iniquity.

2   For they shall soon be cut down like the grass, and wither as the green herb.

3   Trust in the LORD, and do good; so shalt thou dwell in the land, and verily thou shalt be fed.

4   Delight thyself also in the LORD; and He shall give thee the desires of thine heart.

5   Commit thy way unto the LORD; trust also in Him; and He shall bring it to pass.

6   And He shall bring forth thy righteousness as the light, and thy judgment as the noonday.

CP's Signature _____ Date _____

Psalm 100

1   Make a joyful noise unto the LORD, all ye lands.

2   Serve the LORD with gladness: come before His presence with singing.

3 Know ye that the LORD He is God: it is He that hath made us, and not we ourselves; we are His people, and the sheep of His pasture.

4 Enter into His gates with thanksgiving, and into His courts with praise: be thankful unto Him, and bless His name.

5 For the LORD is good; His mercy is everlasting; and His truth endureth to all generations.

CP's Signature _____ Date _____

Psalm 103:1-5

1 Bless the LORD, O my soul: and all that is within me, bless His holy name.

2 Bless the LORD, O my soul, and forget not all His benefits:

3 Who forgiveth all thine iniquities; who healeth all thy diseases;

4 Who redeemeth thy life from destruction; who crowneth thee with loving-kindness and tender mercies;

5 Who satisfieth thy mouth with good things; so that thy youth is renewed like the eagle's.

CP's Signature _____ Date _____

Psalm 119:9-16

9 Wherewithal shall a young man cleanse his way? By taking heed thereto according to Thy word.

10 With my whole heart have I sought thee: O let me not wander from Thy commandments.

11 Thy Word have I hid in mine heart, that I might not sin against Thee.

12 Blessed art Thou, O LORD: teach me Thy statutes.

13 With my lips have I declared all the judgments of Thy mouth.

14 I have rejoiced in the way of Thy testimonies, as much as in all riches.

15 I will meditate in Thy precepts, and have respect unto Thy ways.

16 I will delight myself in Thy statutes: I will not forget Thy Word.

CP's Signature _____ Date _____

Psalm 119:33-40

33 Teach me, O LORD, the way of Thy statutes; and I shall keep it unto the end.

34 Give me understanding, and I shall keep Thy law; yea, I shall observe it with my whole heart.

35 Make me to go in the path of Thy commandments; for therein do I delight.

36 Incline my heart unto Thy testimonies, and not to covetousness.

37 Turn away mine eyes from beholding vanity; and quicken Thou me in Thy way.

38 Stablish Thy Word unto Thy servant, who is devoted to Thy fear.

39 Turn away my reproach which I fear: for Thy judgments are good.

40 Behold, I have longed after Thy precepts: quicken me in Thy righteousness.

CP's Signature _____ Date _____

Appendix:
More Good Things to Know

The 66 Books of the Old & New Testament

I have been teaching the Word of God in Church for almost 30 years. I started teaching Sunday School when I was 13 years old. One of the most common but very obvious hindrances I have observed to teaching any new disciple is their unfamiliarity with the books of the Bible. The Bible is a very large literary work. In reality it is actually 66 books in one book, thus, the word *Bible*.

It is a very good practice to have Bible students memorize the Books of the Kings James Bible, in order. This will give them a strong foundation and reference point when in a Church or Bible Study environment.

I have seen many Christians give up on church assembly or Bible Study, simply because they cannot follow the pastor or teacher when asked to open the Bible. They are very confused when speaking about biblical characters, like Isaiah the prophet or King David. They are not even aware that there is a book called Isaiah or that King David is the primary writer of the book of Psalms.

Hearing about the Scriptures is like sitting for hours hearing a foreign language to new Christians. It can be a very intimidating experience.

Because of this, I have simply listed the names of the Old Testament and New Testament books. This will help every rising disciple of Christ to build on the foundation of the knowledge of the Kingdom of God they are receiving.

39 Books of the Old Testament

Genesis	Ecclesiastes
Exodus	Song of Solomon
Leviticus	Isaiah
Numbers	Jeremiah
Deuteronomy	Lamentations
Joshua	Ezekiel
Judges	Daniel
Ruth	Hosea
1 Samuel	Joel
2 Samuel	Amos
1 Kings	Obadiah
2 Kings	Jonah
1 Chronicles	Micah
2 Chronicles	Nahum
Ezra	Habakkuk
Nehemiah	Zephaniah
Esther	Haggai
Job	Zechariah
Psalms	Malachi
Proverbs	

CP's Signature _____ Date _____

27 Books of the New Testament

Matthew	1 Timothy
Mark	2 Timothy
Luke	Titus
John	Philemon
Acts	Hebrews
Romans	James
1 Corinthians	1 Peter
2 Corinthians	2 Peter
Galatians	1 John
Ephesians	2 John
Philippians	3 John
Colossians	Jude
1 Thessalonians	Revelation
2 Thessalonians	

CP's Signature _____ Date _____

The Romans Road to Salvation

Romans 3:23 – For all have sinned, and come short of the glory of God.

Romans 6:23 – For the wages of sin is death; but the gift of God is eternal life through Jesus Christ our Lord.

Romans 5:8-9 – But God commendeth His love toward us, in that, while we were yet sinners, Christ died for us. Much more then, being now justified by His blood, we shall be saved from wrath through Him.

Romans 10:13 – For whosoever shall call upon the name of the Lord shall be saved.

Romans 10:8-10 – But what saith it? The word is nigh thee, even in thy mouth, and in thy heart: that is, the word of faith, which we preach; that if thou shall confess with thy mouth the Lord Jesus, and shalt believe in thine heart that God hath raised Him from the dead, thou shalt be saved. For with the heart man believeth unto righteousness; and with the mouth confession is made unto salvation.

Romans 12:1-2 – I beseech you therefore, brethren, by the mercies of God, that ye present your bodies a living sacrifice, holy, acceptable unto God, which is your reasonable service. And be not conformed to this world: but be ye transformed by the renewing of your mind, that ye may prove what is that good, and acceptable, and perfect will of God.

CP's Signature _____ Date _____

The Components of the Kingdom

Kingdom Components	The United States of America	The Kingdom of God
King and/or Ruler	The Office of the President	The Lord Jesus Christ
Military	Army, Navy, Airforce, etc.	The Heavenly Host (Angels)
Taxation System	IRS	Tithing
National Land Boundaries	Canada, Mexico, Atlantic & Pacific Oceans, Gulf of Mexico	Heaven & Earth
Laws of the Land	The Constitution	The Word of God
Legislative/ Governing Body	House of Representatives & Senate	The Church (Ecclesia)
Citizens/Subjects	Natural Born Citizens	Born Again Believers
National Native Language(s)	English	Speaking in Tongues
Health Care System	Medicare, Medicaid, ACA	The Gifts of Healing(s)
Prison System	State & Federal Prison	Hell
Governing Offices	Secretary of State, Secretary of Defense, etc.	Apostles, Prophets, etc.

Henderson's 7 Rules of Bible Study

Wisdom is the principal thing; therefore get wisdom: and with all thy getting get understanding. (Proverbs 4:7)

Study to shew thyself approved unto God, a workman that needeth not to be ashamed, rightly dividing the word of truth. (2 Timothy 2:15)

I have received much revelation from the Scriptures. Most of that revelation has been received when I have been willing to accept what the Scriptures say without needing to transpose my preconceived ideas into them.

After the foundation of knowing the location of the books of the Bible has been laid along with the discipline of beginning to meditate and memorize the Word of God, the next step is to begin to understand the Scriptures. Application will come next in the maturation process.

To properly take the necessary step to get understanding of the Word of God, I have noticed that I received the most revelation when following some basic rules of Bible Study, given to me by the Holy Spirit. Over time, these rules have developed into what I now call the "7 Rules of Bible Study."

The more I have been careful to follow these rules, the more I have found that the Scriptures have opened themselves up to me and allowed me to mine the treasures within. These are not the only rules of Bible Study, but I have found them to be quite life-changing in teaching several generations of Bible students to learn how to understand and teach the Word of God.

1) Ask God for Wisdom and Revelation into His Word (Matthew 7:7-8).

I have been studying the Scriptures for over 35 years. There has never been a time when I opened the Bible and asked God to give me Wisdom and Revelation and He failed to do so. I have not always gotten the revelation I wanted, but I have never failed to get the revelation I needed. Only God ultimately knows what the Scriptures mean; thus, it is best to simply ask the Author of the Word of God for Wisdom.

2) Do not interpret the Bible; allow the Word of God to interpret itself (2 Peter 1:20-21).

It is most difficult to stop ourselves from saying "I believe the Scriptures mean ..." or "I think the Bible is saying ..." This is the natural inclination of every Bible student. Most of the time, I have found that the most difficult Scriptural passages tell us what they mean within the context of the same chapter in which they are written. I have received much more revelation from the Word of God by simply being satisfied with the Scriptures' explanation of themselves, instead of inserting my own preconceived ideas into the Word of God.

3) Take the Word of God literally when at all possible.

Christ is the Word (John 1:1). Therefore, the Lord is a master at speaking and writing. Do not assume that a Scripture is symbolic or meant to be taken figuratively, just because it is hard to understand or appears to be harsh, difficult or challenging when taken literally. If Jesus says: *"Whoever looks on a woman to lust after her commits adultery with her in his heart"* or *"If your right eye offends you, pluck it out"* (Matthew 5:28-29), we do not have the right to water down His words because we do not like the implication if they apply to our lives. Jesus meant what He said. If we do not like the result of His commands, we should change our behavior so that His words of judgment will not apply to our lives.

4) Do not add to (or subtract from) the Scriptures.

Be careful not to imagine things in the Scriptures that are not there. For example, there are no modern days of the week in the Scriptures like Monday, Tuesday, Wednesday, etc. We often call Saturday the seventh day, the Sabbath. However, this labeling of the seventh day can cause a misunderstanding of the Scriptures when applied to other Biblical concepts. The Jews had other Sabbaths (such as the Passover) that did not fall on the seventh day of the week. Therefore, teaching that Saturday is the Sabbath would confuse our understanding of the Word of God.

5) Read the Scriptures in Context.

What is the total context of the Scripture you are studying? This includes who, what, when, where, why and how? You cannot isolate a text; it must include the Scriptures around it.

6) Recognize Vertical & Horizontal Truths.

- A Vertical Truth is a promise or command of God that is only applicable for His people at that point in time; it is dispensational. For example: Deuteronomy 14:1-21 is applicable only under the Law. (See, also: Mark 7:19; Acts 10:15; Romans 14).

- A Horizontal Truth is a promise or command of God that is applicable at any time throughout Biblical History. For example: John 15:7; Romans 8:28. A Horizontal Truth is applicable from Genesis to Revelation.

7) **Read the Scriptures afresh every time you open the Bible, especially when you are reading a familiar passage of Scripture.**

Every time you open the Word of God, try to study it as if you have never read it before. Do not try to force the Scriptures to say what you want them to say. Allow God to give you a new revelation every time you read His Word. Wait until you have received a revealed Word of God while studying the Scriptures. Then, compare it to what you already know concerning the Word. Resist the temptation to impose what you already know about the Bible on familiar and unfamiliar Scriptures, alike.

CP's Signature _____ Date _____

Glossary of Bible Words

Abide – Continue without stopping; stay committed (John 15:4-7).

Adoration – Speaking of someone with honor because of who they are and/or what they have done (Hebrews 1:6; Revelation 14:7); worship (Revelation 15:4).

Angels – The military arm of the Kingdom of Heaven called the Heavenly Host or the flames of fire (2 Thessalonians 1:7-8); ministering spirits sent to protect and serve every born-again believer in Jesus Christ (Hebrews 1:14).

Anointing – The burden-removing and yoke-destroying power of God (Isaiah 10:27).

Baptized – Completely immersed or submerged in something [i.e., water (John 4:1-2), the name of Jesus (Acts 2:38), or a teaching (Matthew 28:19-20)].

Begotten – Born, as from a woman, from the womb (John 3:16).

Bible Study – Relentless research of the Scriptures, so as to not leave them until wisdom and understanding are received (2 Timothy 2:15).

Blessed – Prosperous or favored (Luke 1:28, 42; James 1:12).

Carnal – Of this world or limited to the intellect and reasoning of mankind (1 Corinthians 3:1-3).

Chaff – Useless seed coverings and small pieces of stem or leaves that are separated from wheat, barley and other kinds of grain (Psalm 1:4).

Chastisement – Punishment or rebuke (Hebrews 12:6-8).

Church – The Body of Christ (Romans 12:5); the called-out legislative government of the Kingdom of God (Acts 14:23); the many-membered (1 Corinthians 12:14); Holy Ghost-filled, body of believers in Jesus Christ: past, present and future (1 Corinthians 12:13, Hebrews 12:23).

Comfort – To help (2 Corinthians 1:3-4).

Comforter – The Helper, the Holy Ghost, the Holy Spirit (John 14:26).

Commandment – A direct, unsuggested order or law.

Commendeth – Demonstrates or shows (Romans 5:8).

Communion – The Lord's Supper (1 Corinthians 11:20); partaking of the body and blood of Jesus Christ (through bread and wine, respectively) in remembrance of His death until He comes again (1 Corinthians 11:23-30).

Condemnation – A sentence to be discarded or destroyed, because there is no solution for redemption (John 8:10; Titus 2:7-9); a damnation (John 3:19; Romans 8:1).

Confess – To admit or agree from the heart by speaking (Romans 10:9).

Conformed – To be in agreement or pledge allegiance in thought or action (Romans 12:2).

Covenant – A promise or agreement entered by two parties, sealed by blood (Luke 1:72; Romans 11:27; Hebrews 8:6).

Covetousness – Envious desire of something that belongs to someone else (Luke 12:15; Colossians 3:5; Hebrews 13:5).

Crucified – To be executed to death on a cross (Acts 4:10); put to death (Romans 6:6; Galatians 2:20, 5:24).

Debts – Money, goods or services owed (Matthew 6:12, 18:23-35); trespasses (Matthew 6:14-15).

Deliverance – The ministry of being set free from demonic powers and the influence of darkness (Matthew 8:16, 10:1, 8, Mark 16:17, Luke 10:19); to be released from prison or captivity (Matthew 6:13; Luke 4:18).

Demons or Devils – Unclean spirits originating from the Nephilim or Giants of the Old Testament (Genesis 6:4).

Diverse Kinds of Tongues – The gift to speak in one or more languages, unknown to the speaker, natural or spiritual (1 Corinthians 12:10, 14:2; Acts 2:4-11).

Dominion – The state of being fruitful, multiplying, replenishing the earth and subduing it, including all its living creatures and resources (Genesis 1:28); rulership (Romans 6:14; Ephesians 1:21; Jude 1:25; Revelation 1:6).

Edification – The use of words or actions that build, rather than destroy (Romans 15:2; 1 Corinthians 14:3).

Effectual – Persistent action until the effect or result is realized (James 5:16, Philemon 1:6).

Eternal or Everlasting Life – An abundant and prosperous existence that never ends, being outside of the confines of time (John 3:16).

Evidence – Elements of proof or clues that lead to an ultimate solution (Hebrews 11:1).

Exhortation – Words that lift, encourage and persuade (1 Corinthians 14:3; Hebrews 3:13).

Favor – A special gift or blessing above and beyond that which is normally given or made available to others (1 Samuel 2:26; Luke 2:52; Acts 2:47, 7:10).

Fear[1] – To be in terror, dread or an intense state of worry, especially of the unknown or in anticipation of the future (Isaiah 41:10; Luke 8:49-50; 2 Timothy 1:7).

Fear[2] – Alternatively, the "fear of the LORD" is not to be in terror or dread, as we use the word today (Proverbs 9:10); rather, this fear is the attitude of refusing to live your life any other way than according to the Word of God (2 Corinthians 7:1); an attitude stemming from a heart to please the LORD in everything we do (Acts 2:43, 9:31); an attitude or way of thinking the Bible says is the beginning of wisdom (Proverbs 9:10).

Fervent – Diligent (James 5:16; Romans 12:11); burning (2 Peter 3:10-12).

Flesh – Of the carnal mind or physical body (Romans 3:20, 7:18, 8:1-13); the natural part of a man that opposes his spirit (Romans 8:4-5; Galatians 5:16-17).

Fruit of the Spirit – The nine aspects of the "fruit" of the Spirit (Galatians 5:22-23): (1) love, (2) joy, (3) peace, (4) longsuffering, (5) gentleness, (6) goodness, (7) faith, (8) meekness, (9) temperance (see page 138 for greater detail).

Gifts of the Father – The seven operations of God the Father, according to the grace that is given to believers (Romans 12:6–8, 1 Corinthians 12:6). These gifts are given by the operation of the Father and are horizontal endowments, available in the Old & New Testament: (1) prophecy, (2) ministry, (3) teaching, (4) exhortation, (5) giving, (6) ruling, (7) mercy (see page 139 for greater detail).

Gifts of Christ – The four functional office gifts that "Christ gave to the Church" for the perfecting of believers for the work of the ministry to build up the Body of Christ in the unity and knowledge of Jesus, unto the fulness of Christ, exposing deception and ministering truth, stability and maturity to the Body of Christ (Ephesians 4:11-12); sometimes called "The 4-fold Ministry," these office gifts are affirmed, after evidence of such, by the "laying on of hands" (1 Timothy 4:14)(see page 140 for greater detail).

Gifts of the Holy Spirit – The nine diversities of gifts or manifestations of the Holy Spirit (1 Corinthians 12:4,7); given for the common good (Acts 1:8; 1 Corinthians 12:8-10): (1) word of wisdom, (2) word of knowledge, (3) faith, (4) gifts of healing, (5) working of miracles, (6) prophecy, (7) discerning of spirits, (8) divers kinds of tongues, (9) interpretation of tongues (see page 141 for greater detail).

Glory – The state of righteous boasting or honor (2 Corinthians 5:12); the illumination of one's inner-righteousness and holiness (Matthew 17:1-2; Romans 2:10, 15:17).

Grace – Unearned favor or kindness, unmerited gift (Ephesians 2:8-9); special abundance or blessing, provision (2 Corinthians 9:8, 12:9); a time of forgiveness, as with debt (Ephesians 1:7); a grace period.

Griefs – Sicknesses, diseases or infirmities (Isaiah 53:4).

Hallowed – Holy (Luke 11:2).

Healing – The healthcare system of the Kingdom of God (1 Corinthians 12:28); the process of making something or someone whole inside or outside (Luke 4:18); making the inner and outer man whole without sickness, disease, infirmity or mental fragmentation (Psalm 103:3, 147:3); gift of the Holy Spirit (1 Corinthians 12:9).

Heart – The part of the mind or soul that reflects who we are when no one is watching (Jeremiah 17:9); one's true inner-self or thought process (Matthew 12:33-35).

Hope – An expectation that a promise will be fulfilled (Titus 2:13); the ultimate dream or vision (Romans 4:18, 5:3-5).

Husbandman – A vinedresser (Genesis 9:20); one who tends, prunes and maintains vineyards (John 15:1-2).

Inheritance – Wealth (land, money, knowledge, etc.) passed on to another, usually to the next generation, due to a death in a family (Proverbs 13:22).

Iniquities – Generational sins (Deuteronomy 5:9; Romans 4:7).

Intercession – Standing in the gap or praying for someone with the same urgency you would want someone to pray for you if you were in trouble, dire need or in an emergency (Romans 8:26-27, 34).

Judgment – A sentence or reward handed down by a higher authority (2 Corinthians 5:10).

Justified – To be reinstated into right-standing before God because of the sacrifice of Christ (Romans 5:1, 9); when God has made it **just-as-if-I'd** never sinned (1 Corinthians 6:11).

Kingdom – The place where the King has supreme rule, dominion and authority (1 Corinthians 15:24).

Law – The constitution of the nation of Israel in the Old Testament established by Moses the patriarch (Exodus 31:18); the preamble of that constitution known as The Ten Commandments (Exodus 20:2-17); the spoken or written statutes, precepts and commandments of God for righteous living in His Kingdom (Hebrews 10:16).

Liberty – Freedom (Galatians 5:1; 2 Corinthians 3:17).

Literal – The unadulterated, original or unchanged version; to take "as is".

Meditate – To set aside time to think about something with the intent to remember and make it a part of one's normal behavior (Joshua 1:8; Psalm 1:2).

Obedient – Following the set rule(s) or order(s) (Isaiah 1:19); fulfilling the Law (Exodus 24:7).

Observation – The act of looking with an intent to find in the natural and not the spiritual realm (Luke 17:20-21).

Petitions – Earnest requests in the presence of the Father in Heaven (1 John 5:15).

Porter – A watcher or gatekeeper (John 10:2-3).

Power[1] – Authority (Matthew 9:6; 1 Corinthians 4:20); the ability to command another (Luke 10:19).

Power[2] – The force necessary to move an obstacle (Acts 1:8); the ability to transfer supernatural energy from one thing to another (Luke 9:1); virtue (Luke 6:19).

Prayer – Communication or intimate communion with God [through adoration, confession, thanksgiving and supplication] (Ephesians 6:18; Philippians 4:6; 1 Timothy 2:1); the act of believing [by faith] in the promises of God through asking and speaking to the Father (Matthew 21:22); any declaration or decree by faith (James 5:15).

Precepts – Must-have mandates or commandments (Psalm 119:27).

Principality – Most commonly, one of the fallen angels that rule over a city, region, nation or some other territory (Ephesians 6:12); one of God's prince angels such as the archangel Michael or Gabriel (Daniel 10:13, Ephesians 1:20-21).

Propitiation – Atoning sacrifice, payment for wrongdoing (Romans 3:25); acceptable substitute (1 John 2:2).

Prosper – To be elevated, promoted or increased in wealth (3 John 1:2).

Prudent – Wise and calculating (Proverbs 12:23; 1 Corinthians 1:19).

Redeemer – One who pays for the life of another to set them free from captivity or imprisonment (Isaiah 49:26).

Regeneration – The growth of new cells or substance after the original have died (Titus 3:5); the act of creating again (Matthew 19:28).

Reign – To have dominion (2 Timothy 2:12); to rule as a king (Psalm 96:10).

Remission – A washing away, cleansing, releasing or forgiveness of debt, sin or trespasses (Matthew 26:28; Luke 1:77; Hebrews 9:22).

Repent – To change the mind (Matthew 21:29; Luke 17:3); a 180-degree change of thought and behavior (Luke 3:8).

Resurrection – Awakening or rising from the dead (John 11:24-25; Acts 24:15).

Righteousness – The state of being right or to be in right standing with God (2 Corinthians 5:21); God's way of being right or correct (Romans 3:21); the position of lining-up according to the Word of God (Romans 1:17).

Sabbath – The day or season of rest ordained by the Lord (Exodus 16:23-25); the Jews had Sabbath days, weeks, months and years (Colossians 2:16); the Year of Jubilee is a

Sabbath year (Lev. 25:1-7); the seventh day is commonly known as the Sabbath (Exodus 20:8-11); Jesus is the Sabbath (Hebrews 4:1-11).

Sacrifice – Something disposed of or terminated in lieu of something else (Leviticus 1:1-17; Ephesians 5:2; Hebrews 5:1).

Salvation (Saved) – Deliverance or rescue (Genesis 49:18; Psalm 37:39); preserved or restored back to the original position or state (Psalm 14:7; Luke 1:76-77); God has saved us from the penalty of sin (Acts 4:12; Romans 1:16, 6:23), and has caused us to be seated in heavenly places with Christ Jesus (Ephesians 2:6); when we are saved, we regain the original authority that God gave Adam in the beginning, to rule and reign over the earth (Genesis 1:26-28; John 1:12).

Scornful – Those who hate and mock the behavior of the just (Psalm 1:1; Proverbs 29:8).

Shepherd – A watchman and keeper of sheep (Luke 2:8; John 10:14).

Signs – Witnesses or proofs that something is legitimate or real (Mark 16:17-18; 2 Corinthians 12:12).

Sorrow – Pain and anxiety (Isaiah 53:3-4; Revelation 21:4).

Soul – The part of a human being that holds the body and spirit together, comprised of the mind, will and emotions (Genesis 2:7; Mark 12:30; 1 Thessalonians 5:23; Hebrews 4:12).

Sound Mind – Undivided thoughts or imagination (2 Corinthians 10:4-5); able to make wise decisions without turning back from them later because they seem difficult to perpetuate (2 Timothy 1:7); single-minded, the opposite of double-minded (James 1:8).

Statutes – Written laws that limit the boundaries of an activity or behavior used to pass judgment (Exodus 15:26).

Stripes – Punishment by whips and lashings (Proverbs 19:29; 2 Corinthians 11:24); punishment that Jesus took upon His body, while on the way to the crucifixion (1 Peter 2:24).

Substance – The basic building blocks or ingredients of a larger, complete, or whole thing (Luke 15:13; Hebrews 11:1).

Sup – To dine with the intent to develop an intimate personal relationship (Luke 17:8; Revelation 3:20).

Supplication – An earnest request, especially without taking "No" for an answer (1 Kings 8:44-45); the begging or pleading for an extension of favor (Ephesians 6:18; Philippians 4:6).

Testimonies – The many stories, witnesses or accounts that prove an event occurred (Deuteronomy 6:20-25).

Tithe – 10 percent of one's substance, increase or prosperity (Malachi 3:8-10).

Transformed – Renewed and completely changed (Romans 12:2); to be metamorphosized (2 Corinthians 11:14-15).

Transgressions – The sins of breaking the Law (Psalm 32:5).

Truth – The Word of God (John 8:32; 14:6; 17:17; 1 Thessalonians 2:13).

Understanding – The confident knowledge of a subject with the ability to practically explain it to others (Luke 1:3, 24:45).

Ungodly – Against or in opposition to God (Psalm 1:1, 4-5; Proverbs 16:27; Jude 1:4, 14-19).

Wages – Cost, penalty or payment (John 4:36; Romans 6:23).

Wealth – Amassed substance, often monetary, devoid of lack or poverty (Psalm 112:1-3; Proverbs 13:11).

Worship – To give completely of oneself for the adoration and service of another (Psalm 29:2, 86:9; Matthew 4:10; Romans 1:25).

Yoked – To be connected together for the purpose of carrying a burden or weight (Amos 3:3; 2 Corinthians 6:14).

The Fruit of the Spirit

There are nine aspects of the "fruit" of the Spirit, as listed in Galatians 5:22-23.

Love – Charity or benevolence (1 Corinthians 13:1-13); the unconditional dedication and compassion that can only be released from the heart of God Himself (John 3:16); the ability to give of oneself for the sole benefit or profit of another (John 15:13).

Joy – The prosperity and abundant resources entered into or received from the Kingdom of God (Psalm 16:11; Hebrews 12:2); happiness or fulfillment derived from one's connection to the Almighty (Nehemiah 8:10; Acts 13:52).

Peace – The state of being still or at rest with no thought of calamity, to cease from war (John 14:27).

Longsuffering – Patient or slow-to-anger (2 Peter 3:9); waiting without anxiety or stress (Romans 9:22-23).

Gentleness – Kindness (Colossians 3:12); a favor or disinterested gift for the benefit of another (1 Thessalonians 2:7).

Goodness – Doing what is right in respect to others or doing right by others (Romans 12:9, 15:14).

Faith – Finishing what one has started believing, especially when trials or afflictions occur (Mark 25:21). The ability to press through; persistence and longevity of believing, good stewardship or faithfulness (1 Corinthians 4:2).

Meekness – Submissive humility (Ephesians 4:2); yielding my rights (1 Corinthians 9:1-27; Philippians 2:1-8).

Temperance – Self-control, the ability to govern oneself; internal government (2 Peter 2:9-10).

Gifts from God

There are three main categories of gifts that God gives to believers and the Church: (I) Gifts of the Father (Romans 12:6–8), (II) Gifts of Christ (Ephesians 4:11), and (III) Gifts of the Holy Spirit (1 Corinthians 12:8-10).

1. The Gifts of the Father

These are seven appointed gifts that differ in each believer, according to the grace that is given (Romans 12:6–8). One or more of these gifts is individually delegated to believers to love, honor and prefer one another in kindness (Romans 12:4, 10; James 3:17).

(1) **Prophecy** – A gift to speak with forthrightness and insight (Acts 2:17; Romans 12:6; Revelation 19:10).

(2) **Ministry/Serving** – A gift to humbly serve others in the Body of Christ (Matthew 20:25-26; Romans 12:7).

(3) **Teaching** – A gift to illuminate divine truths received from God (Romans 12:7; 1 Corinthians 14:19; 2 Timothy 2:2).

(4) **Exhortation** – A gift to lift-up and encourage others; to comfort or console, (Acts 20:2; Romans 12:8; 1 Timothy 4:13); to herald.

(5) **Giving** – A gift to give cheerfully, helping those who are without (Romans 12:8; 2 Corinthians 8:2; 9:7); especially monetarily.

(6) **Ruling/Leadership** – A gift to diligently lead, to go first, to show the way by example (Romans 12:8; 1 Timothy 5:17; 1 Peter 5:3); to organize or be a chief administrator (Daniel 6:1-4); to wield power and execute righteous dominion.

(7) **Mercy** – A gift to cheerfully relate to others in empathy, respect and honesty in their suffering (Matthew 5:7; Romans 12:8; James 2:13; Micah 6:8).

2. The Gifts of Christ

The four office grace gifts that "Christ gave to the Church" for the perfecting of believers for the work of the ministry to build up the Body of Christ in the unity and knowledge of Jesus, unto the fulness of Christ, exposing deception and ministering truth, stability and maturity to the Body of Christ (Ephesians 4:11-12). Sometimes called "The 4-fold Ministry," these office gifts are affirmed, after evidence of such, by the "laying on of hands" (1 Timothy 4:14).

(1) **Apostle** – A special messenger or sent one (Luke 11:49); one of the grace gifts of the administration of Jesus Christ assigned to build the Church (Ephesians 4:11-12); apostles are given the ability to cast out demons and heal sicknesses and diseases (Luke 9:1-6, 10); these are the gifts of discerning of spirits and gifts of healings, respectively (1 Corinthians 12:9-10); they are to use these gifts to stand against the Kingdom of Darkness, just as the kings and judges did in the Old Testament (Acts 26:16-18); the apostles are commissioned to do what Jesus would do if He were physically here today (Ephesians 2:20); apostles operate in signs, wonders and miracles (Acts 2:43; 2 Corinthians 12:12) and tend to operate in the other three offices, broadly, as demonstrated throughout the New Testament.

(2) **Prophet** – A seer or one who sees clearly into the spiritual realm to inquire of God (1 Samuel 9:9); one of the grace gifts of the administration of Jesus Christ assigned to build the Church (Ephesians 4:11-12); the prophet is the official mouthpiece or Press Secretary of

the Kingdom of God (Ephesians 2:20; Revelation 19:10); the prophet is assigned to speak as if God Himself were speaking (Romans 16:25-26); the prophets also operate by dreams and visions and are able to interpret them (Numbers 12:6; Acts 2:17).

(3) **Evangelist** – A herald, a preacher (2 Timothy 4:1-5); one of the grace gifts of the administration of Jesus Christ assigned to build the Church (Ephesians 4:11-12); the evangelist specifically leads God's people by preaching the Gospel of the Kingdom and of Jesus Christ (also called the Gospel of Peace), and moves in healing, miracles, signs and wonders, bringing many to salvation (Acts 8:5-7; Romans 10:14-15).

(4) **Pastor-Teacher** – A shepherd, someone that leads and feeds the flock of God by the Word of God (Acts 20:28); one of the grace gifts of the administration of Jesus Christ assigned to build the Church (Ephesians 4:11-12); the pastor specifically leads God's people by teaching them with the knowledge of the Word until understanding is achieved (Jeremiah 3:15).

3. The Gifts of the Holy Spirit

The nine diversities of gifts or manifestations of the Holy Spirit (1 Corinthians 12:4,7) that empower the believer to witness, given for the common good (Acts 1:8; 1 Corinthians 12:8-10).

(1) **Word of Wisdom** – The gift to give a Word from God that tells us what to do or how something will happen (1 Corinthians 12:8; James 3:17).

(2) **Word of Knowledge** – The gift to give information about a person or thing that would be unique or of significant

interest to the person hearing it (John 4:16-19, 28-29; 1 Corinthians 12:8).

(3) **Faith** – The gift of power to remove obstacles (Matthew 8:26, 17:20; Mark 11:22-24; John 18:6; 1 Corinthians 12:9; Hebrews 11:6).

(4) **Gifts of Healing** – The gifts to cure and eliminate sickness and disease (1 Corinthians 12:9, 28).

(5) **Working of Miracles** – The gift to defy the laws of nature or physics, such as turning water to wine or walking on water (Matthew 14:24-29; John 2:1-11, 6:2; Acts 2:43, 6:8; 1 Corinthians 12:10).

(6) **Prophecy** – A gift to enable forthtelling of the past, present or future (1 Corinthians 12:10, 14:31; 2 Peter 1:21).

(7) **Discerning of Spirits** – The gift to understand what spirit beings are in operation (1 Corinthians 12:10), used primarily by Jesus and His disciples in the New Testament to cast out demons (Acts 16:16-18).

(8) **Divers Kinds of Tongues** – The gift to give a message or prayer in a language unknown to the speaker or hearer (Romans 8:26; 1 Corinthians 12:10, 14:15).

(9) **Interpretation of Tongues** – The gift to understand and translate what is said in a language unknown to the speaker or hearer (1 Corinthians 12:10).

Other Great Kingdom Resources
by Larry Henderson, Jr.

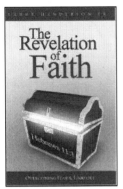

The Revelation of Faith reveals the fundamental teachings of Jesus Christ concerning the supernatural power of faith. In this book you will embark upon a journey to discover this radical kind of faith: faith that moves mountains, faith that raises the dead, faith that destroys sickness and disease, faith that feeds the multitudes, faith that clothes the homeless, faith that walks on water, faith that evangelizes thousands in one day, faith that snatches our families from the clutches of the enemy, faith that pleases God.

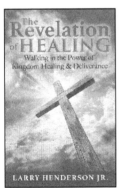

The Revelation of Healing is a concise volume to train and equip the saints to walk in the power of supernatural healing and deliverance. It is a clear guide to teach every Christian how to get delivered from Generational Curses, Habitual Sins, receive healing from Sickness & Disease, release from Demonic Oppression, and relief from pain, anxiety, and sorrows. The Revelation of Healing reveals the life-changing truth that the sacrifice of Jesus Christ on the Cross was given equally to forgive our sins and heal our bodies. It proves this truth is as relevant today as it was almost 2000 years ago.

Order on Amazon!

Kingdom Courses

The Kingdom Institute (KI) is a teaching and training school commissioned to build, develop and equip leaders to advance the Kingdom of God. The KI consists of multiple 16-week courses that teach and activate students in the Kingdom areas of Prayer and Bible Study, Understanding Spiritual Gifts, Healing and Deliverance, Prophecy, Power Evangelism, Executive Leadership, Strategic Management and many other topics.

The Kingdom Institute is also the Ministry License and Ordination arm of the Kingdom Advancement Center.

Each of our courses are comprehensive and allow each student to grow as the Spirit of the Lord allows. Foundational topics in our courses include but are not limited to:

Kingdom Foundations (KF100)

- The Established Habit of Bible Study
- Understanding the Kingdom
- The Established Habit of Prayer
- Salvation & Eternal Life
- Activating Our Faith
- Prophecy & Tongues
- Understanding Spiritual Gifts
- The Revelation of Healing
- Experiencing Deliverance

Kingdom Foundations (KF200)

- How to Study the Bible
- Kingdom & Dominion
- Prayer & Fasting
- Evangelism & Prophecy
- Faith vs. Fear (Unbelief)
- The Fruit of the Spirit
- 4-Fold Ministry
- Healing & Words of Knowledge
- Angels & Prophetic Healing Teams

Teaching Foundations (TF300)

- Bible Expository Methods
- Grab Bag Teaching Game
- KF100 Teaching Seminar 1-2
- Lesson Plan Teaching Strategy
- Lesson Plan Seminar 1-4
- Teaching Seminar 1-4

Evangelism Foundations (EF300)

- Salvation & Eternal Life
- Defending Your Faith: Apologetics
- Understanding How to Evangelize 1-4
- Prophetic Evangelism
- Office of Evangelist
- Writing Your Testimony
- Mobilizing the Church for Evangelism

Prophecy Foundations (PF300)

- The Prophetic Kingdom
- Dreams & Visions
- The Spirit of Prophecy & the Office of Prophet
- Prophetic Character
- Naba Prophesying
- Word of Wisdom & Word of Knowledge
- Intercessory Prayer
- Decrees & Declarations

Kingdom Institute (KI)
Registration and Programming

MONDAY:
- Registration begins at 6:30 PM
- Class begins at 7:00 PM

WEDNESDAY:
- No Registration on Wednesdays (only Mondays)
- Class begins at 7:00 PM

To request Apostle Henderson or another KI Minister to plan a Conference, Seminar or Kingdom Course in your area, please call or email to arrange a program to fit your ministry's needs:

ki@thekingdomac.com
www.thekingdomac.com
(312) 473-5740

About the Author

Larry Henderson is the Senior Overseer, apostle, pastor-teacher and co-founder of The Kingdom Advancement Center in Elgin, Illinois. He is the author of *The Revelation of Healing: Walking in the Power of Kingdom Healing & Deliverance* and *The Revelation of Faith: Overcoming Fear & Unbelief.*

Larry and his wife, Prophet Tiffany Henderson, are also serving the Body of Christ together through the Kingdom Advancement Apostolic Ministers Network (KAAMN). Larry and Tiffany reside in the Northwest Suburbs of Chicago, Illinois with their two children.

To request Apostle Henderson or another Minister from The Kingdom Institute (KI) to plan a Conference, Seminar or Kingdom Course in your area, please call or email to arrange a program to fit your ministry's needs:

ki@thekingdomac.com
www.thekingdomac.com
(312) 473-5740

Made in the USA
Lexington, KY
18 June 2019